READING
KETCHUP

AND OTHER ESSAYS

TIM MILLER

GNATCATCHER
PRESS

Published by Gnatcatcher Press 2022
San Marcos, CA, USA

So Ben, what I don't think you can do is buy this book and then give it to Marty inside another form of binding, like a turkey sandwich slathered with that Durkee Famous sauce we used to use. While I might appreciate Marty biting into a sandwich that is actually my book, I'm pretty sure it would run afoul of copyright laws. Maybe add really hot jalapeños instead?

ISBN PAPERBACK: 979-8-9863358-5-8

ISBN EBOOK: 979-8-9863358-6-5

CONTENTS

READING KETCHUP   1

THE QUINTESSENTIAL PEARL JAM ALBUM FOR ALIENS   27

WITH OR WITHOUT YOU   45

SOS IN THE JURY LOUNGE   65

BORBORYGMI   85

HISTORIC(!) RUGBY   119

SOS IN THE JURY LOUNGE 2   131

Also by Tim Miller

Spooves

If the complexities and contradictions from Hamlet *and* King Lear *can be spelled out on the stage, then everything is possible.*

—Paraphrased from
John Russel's *Meanings of Modern Art*

READING KETCHUP

It might be interesting to learn more about the collaborative relationship between James Patterson and Dolly Parton for the March 2022 release of the novel *Run, Rose, Run*. No disrespect intended (I love me some Dolly), but it might be like reading a story written by a sixth grader. It *might* be interesting. But it might not.

Far more interesting to me is the question and on-going debate in literary circles: Is James Patterson a Hero or a Villain? Not all that long ago, I decided to try and find out.

$$a = NYPD\ RED\ 2$$

Usually, when someone gives me a book, I read it. This habit is a combination of superstition and compulsion. As if the book fell from the sky, like I was *meant* to read this book and it has a particular message for me at this exact moment in my life. Something like that.

For example, once upon a time I was an English as a Second Language teacher at an adult school. Near the end of the semester a student gave me *The Smoke Jumper* by Nicolas Evans as a gift. The book didn't strike me as particularly appealing, yet until I read it, every time I regarded it on my shelf, it seemed to blink like an old-school answering machine: "I have a message for you!"

So one evening over appetizers, when my father-in-law handed me *NYPD RED 2* by James Patterson (with Marshall Karp), I once again felt the Call of the Books from the Sky—or whatever it is I feel. "It's good," my father-in-law said, possibly referring to the mango salsa.

Glancing at the blue paperback cover, I read, "KIDNAPPING. TORTURE. MURDER. ONLY NYPD RED CAN HANDLE NEW YORK'S MOST SENSATIONAL CASES." The thriller genre is not my go-to, but perhaps part of why I read Books From the Sky is that, as an aspiring writer, I try to follow the advice of Stephen King and William Faulkner: essentially, "Read everything." Also, I had never read a James Patterson book. I noted that the cover included the phrase, "THE WORLD'S #1 BEST SELLING WRITER."

On the inside of the cover were three pages of "RAVES FOR JAMES PATTERSON'S SIZZLING NEW SERIES!" On the back of the cover were the words, "THE EXPLOSIVE #1 BESTSELLER #1 New York Times #1 Chicago Tribune #1 Publishers Weekly #1 Entertainment Weekly #1 USA Today and #4 Wall Street Journal."

Then I glanced at his author bio to see that he had sold 300 million books. (Turn the page to today, and that number is closer to 425 million.)

Standing in my father-in-law's kitchen munching grapes, I took a moment and fathomed that: 300 million people. And while I dimly recognized that 300 million books sold didn't necessarily mean 300 individual readers, it was too late— my imagination had latched onto that number and I was off. I imagined all these people together, in one place (like some humongous stadium), reading. Then I envisioned *only one person* writing the books in front of all those faces. Like I sometimes do, I took it one step too far and tried to conceive of myself as that person. Everything froze, like a little wheel spinning in my head.

"Thanks," I said to my father-in-law, turning to the cheese tray. "I need something to read on our upcoming trip."

A month later, I was about fifty pages from the end (I was reading other things too, OK?) and, to put it simply, I was less than enthralled with the story. Despite nearing the climax of the action, I wasn't too eager to find out whether they found the Hazmat Killers, if the lead detective got together with his partner or his shrink girlfriend, what happened with the partner's drug addict husband, and how the NYC mayoral election turned out.

Instead, I was keen to find out what had perplexed me before I started reading. Something didn't add up. It was a problem of logic that can be expressed mathematically: if $a=b$ and $b=c$, then $a=c$. This is known as transitivity in mathematics. Transitivity of one relation to another is so natural that way back Euclid stated it as the first of his Common Notions (you can practically hear the "duh"): Things that are equal to the same thing are also equal to one another.

It follows:

$$a = b$$
$$NYPD\ RED\ 2 = \text{James Patterson}$$

$$b = c$$
$$\text{James Patterson} = 300\text{ million readers}$$

$$a = c$$
$$NYPD\ RED\ 2 = 300\text{ million readers}$$

• • •

Whatever the real number is, millions and millions of people have read, essentially, books of the same style and substance as *NYPD RED 2*. (For the purpose of this essay, let's call it a cool 300 hundred mill.) After Patterson, or Karp, resolved the tension and tied up the loose ends, I skipped the "exciting preview" of another Patterson thriller and went back to the equations like an ancient mathematician refusing to be stumped.

I wanted to test them, tease them out, examine them under strong light and magnification, and follow my curiosity down the rabbit hole. Perhaps, if I worked at the sides of the equations, boiled them down and distilled the components, then I might learn whether this behemoth of an author stands on the side of Good or Evil.

One afternoon while the kids were asleep, I dusted off my journalism hat and started digging. The first thing I wrote down in my notebook was: "Buy a real journalism hat." The second thing was this quote from legal thriller writer Liza Scottoline: "50 million Elvis Presley fans couldn't be wrong and JP makes 50 million look like a good start."

Maybe my essay was over before it started. The little wheel in my head started spinning again, freezing me with the thought of 50 million people— *as a start*. I was about to leave it and move on to *The Smoke Jumper* when I read this quote from JP. "If you want to write for a lot of people, think about them a little bit. What do they like? What are their needs? A lot of people in this country go through their days numb. They need to be entertained. They need to feel something."

Those last two sentences rattled in my head for a moment as my first stumbling block. I had never thought of entertainment as a need before, but JP is right. You can climb straight up Maslow's pyramid, from physiological needs, past safety, love, and esteem, to where it sits at the very top as part of self-actualization.

Way back when, people were finding stories in the stars. Fast-forward to today and entertainment ranks fourth in consumer spending, right after housing, food, and healthcare. That's part of $c = 300$ **million**. People need to be entertained (ahem), even by essays. That's why we spend hundreds of billions of dollars on it every year. Take say, 2004, when Americans spent $705.9 billion on entertainment alone, the equivalent of the gross national product of Canada.

• • •

I tipped my pretend hat back with satisfaction: I was getting somewhere. Entertainment is a need and to fill this need people buy JP books that, on one hand, are "accessible and engaging" (according to the Hero JP), and, on the other hand, are generally about sociopaths, sadism, rape, kidnapping, sex, gruesome murders and graphic violence (hiss, hiss, Villain JP).

Next questions: Do Americans really *need* to feel all this? Do Americans *need* to read about a person being burned alive or a live snake being fed into a victim's anus? Do Americans *need* a story about a missing president? (Well, that one's a can of worms.) I went back to the equations.

Books and reading might equal esteem and self-actualization, but it seemed incongruous that people are reading *NYPD RED 2* to feel good. I realized I was at a fork in the essay. Down one path was $b = $ JP, the WORLD'S BESTSELLING AUTHOR. And the other path was $c = 300$ million readers. Like maybe it's not JP, but us, collectively. We just need a good story from a trusted source.

I dug at the two tunnels like a mole, getting deeper and deeper, until I emerged suddenly on JP's couch in Palm Beach, with his wife serving cookies to extensions of myself: wannabe writers.

I can't picture 300 million people, but I can *smell* this: his wife serving aspiring writers chocolate chip cookies as the face on the back of all those hard covers speaks comfortably, in golf attire, with a hint of disdain.

b = James Patterson

The term "juggernaut" may not even do him justice. The sheer volume of his career is staggering. He has sold an estimated 425 million books. He has published over 200 novels and counting. He has appeared on the *New York Times* Best-Sellers list 114 times. Of these appearances on the B.S. list, 67 different times he has been #1. He had a stretch of 19 consecutive books make the B.S. list. The genres engulfed by his writing include crime/thrillers (his bread and butter), science fiction, romance, "women's weepies," graphic novels, young adult, nonfiction, golf, and even Christmas-themed books. Since 2006, 1 in 17 hardcover books sold was by JP. He has ten different series of books. In recent years, he has sold more books than Dan Brown, John Grisham, and Stephen King *combined*.

In 2010 he signed a seventeen-book deal, which he quickly surpassed. (A deal like that, for me, right now, would be the writing equivalent of La Sagrada Familia—sorry if that's an obscure reference.) Since 2010, he has released more than ten books a year. His publisher is Little, Brown, & Co., a division of Hachette Book Group. JP is responsible for roughly thirty percent of their revenues. He has two editors and three full-time Hachette employees, including a brand-manager, a marketing director, and a sales manager. Presumably, there's also a small militia of assistants for all that coffee.

Then there's the much publicized co-writers, of which JP has about two dozen who he sends outlines to and which now includes a former president. JP is apparently "intimately involved" with the publication of each book. According to Brown Michael Pietsch, his editor and publisher at Little, "Jim is at the very least co-publisher of his own books."

He may be at the very least the co-publisher, but how much is he the writer of say, *NYPD RED 2*, my first JP novel? There's no way of knowing.

What we do know all about is the process. He has been forthcoming about it in both in the *New York Times* and *Vanity Fair*. Basically, he has an overstuffed folder bulging with ideas that are constantly sprouting from the fecundity of his imagination. He picks up an idea and writes by hand a detailed outline on a legal pad. Then he hires someone, "often a former colleague from his advertising days to write the ensuing scenes—usually in 30- to 40-page chunks." He reviews the pages, sometimes providing notes and other times rewriting the work entirely.

His format: lots of periods in each paragraph, lots of paragraphs on each page, and a paucity of pages in each chapter. The idea is that the pages start to turn themselves. Description and background are basically non-existent. There is minimal scene or character development. The emphasis is instead firmly placed on the story, the pace of the plot, and what *happens* to the characters.

He has gone from a writer with a process to something like a CEO in charge of a streamlined system, a massive assembly-line machine that churns out book after book. This is how he produces so many books and makes over $80 million each year. JP dislikes the assembly line comparison, yet he also looks at publishing books the way "Henry Ford would look at it." This example is the first of many contradictions, ironies, and paradoxes regarding JP as a man who wants things both ways, like donating to independent bookstores while simultaneously writing books that essentially contribute to putting them out of business.

The critics can yell until they are blue in the face. English professors can groan about him being compared to Charles Dickens. Stephen King can call him something worse than "terrible writer"—which he did. He could call him (pause for dramatic effect) an "airport author" —which he hasn't, but which is a real JP bristler.

And, really, what can a critic (or essayist, for that matter) say or do in the face of such astonishing success? Be bitter? Accuse him of pandering to the masses, churning out schlock? Say that he's dumbing America down?

JP might bristle, depending on where the criticism comes from, but more times than not he just gives a wry smile because he knows, deep within himself, that he is a storyteller, a competent one, who has "made a lot of people happy." Millions of people, actually, and that doesn't include cheapies like myself who just use the library or read Books From the Sky. Nothing a critic can do or say puts a dent in 400 million books sold. It's like pissing into a hurricane.

There are plenty of other staggering statistics regarding his career, like according to *Forbes* he is the seventh-highest paid celebrity in the world, ahead of LeBron James and Taylor Swift. But for b = JP, these other stats don't really matter since we have c = 300 million. Rather, the focus is on JP, who he is, how he got there, and what he represents.

This writer would be curious to know how JP would approach

telling his own story. Apparently, *James Patterson by James Patterson,* the memoir published in 2022 tells lots of stories from his life, but manages to leave out *his* story. It's not likely he'll write a traditional autobiography in his characteristic style, but if he did it might go something like this:

CHAPTER 1

I was born in 1947 in Newburgh, New York. Growing up I wandered the woods and told stories. At 19, I got a job at a psychiatric hospital and took the night shift, where I started reading in earnest. I went to school and graduated *summa cum laude* twice—first with a BA in English from Manhattan College and then with an MA in English from Vanderbilt University.

CHAPTER 2

I realized that if I became a college professor I would kill my love of reading and writing. I went to New York and became a junior copywriter at J. Walter Thompson.
I read a lot of heavy hitters. My main takeaway was: "I am not capable of this."

CHAPTER 3

Then, while working in advertising I read commercial books like *The Exorcist* and *The Day of the Jackal.* My two main take-aways from these books were: "I like this, and I can do this."
   I bought a typewriter.

CHAPTER 4

My first book, *The Thomas Berryman Number,* was rejected by over thirty publishers before Little, Brown finally bought it for $8,500. No one came to the first book signing, which

took place at the World Trade Center, except my girlfriend.
The book sold something like 10,000 copies (pretty good for a
debut) and won the prestigious Edgar Award for a first novel
from the Mystery Writers of America.

CHAPTER 5

It was the '70s. I continued working at advertising like a madman.

I published three more novels, including one that I currently
tell people not to read called *The Season of the Machete*.

CHAPTER 6

My girlfriend developed a brain tumor and died. I stopped
writing. My blood pressure and I went up the corporate ladder.
I came up with the slogan "I'm a Toys'R'Us Kid," and became
the CEO of North American operations.

CHAPTER 7

Somewhere around 1985, I began writing again. On my next
book, I decided it's better bare bones than fleshed out. This
allowed me to get directly to the story without getting bogged
down in sentences.

I evolved this style further with my next book, my first to
land on the B.S. list, *Along Came a Spider*.

CHAPTER 8

I kept my day job with a sign on the door that said, "Surprise
me." In 1996, I started writing full-time and wrote a golf book
with a friend. I liked working with other people. In 1997, I got
married. I plugged steadily along for the next few years, mostly
writing the hit detective series about Alex Cross.

CHAPTER 9

In 2001, I started another series, *The Woman's Murder Club,* and over the next twenty years my career took off, churning out books, adding more series, branching out into young adult fiction and other genres, and piling on co-authors. I've told some great stories and made a lot of people happy. And I don't plan on stopping any time soon.

The end.

• • •

This table shows the runaway train that is JP's publishing career.

Approximate Number of Books Published by James Patterson by Year

(Starting in 2016, I include "Bookshots," short stories or novellas—the brainchild of the Villain JP?)

(Also, ~ = about)

Year	Books Published	Estimated Co-Authors
1976	1	0
1977	1	0
1978	0	0
1979	1	0
1980	1	0
1981	0	0
1982	0	0
1983	0	0

1984	0	0
1985	0	0
1986	1	0
1987	0	0
1988	0	0
1989	1 Developed colloquial storytelling with *The Midnight Club*	0
1990	0	0
1991	0	0
1992	1 *Along Came a Spider:* First NY Times Best Seller	0
1993	0	0
1994	0	0
1995	1	1
1996	3	1
1997	1	0
1998	1	0
1999	1	0
2000	1	0
2001	3	0
2002	3	2
2003	2	1
2004	5	2
2005	5	3
2006	5	3
2007	6	3
2008	7	3
2009	9	6
2010	10	6
2011	11	8
2012	14	8
2013	13	8

2014	16	12
2015	17	11
2016	~50	~33
2017	~55	~40
2018	~25	~20 *(including Bill Clinton)*
2019	~20	~15
2020	~25	~15
2021	~20	~10

In the course of wearing my pretend-journalism hat and doing all this research, I thought I stumbled on the secret to JP's success in the form of a nonfiction publication entitled *The Day America Told the Truth: What People Really Believe About Everything That Really Matters.*

This is the work he released just before *Along Came a Spider*, so it carries the implication that this study helped JP truly know and understand his readers' deepest desires and fears. JP and his co-author, Peter Kim, claimed that their survey of over 5,000 people revealed hidden truths about God, sex, family and politics. Things like: twenty-five percent of people would leave their family for $10 million, twenty-three percent would be a prostitute for a week for the same sum, and seven percent of people would kill a stranger for $10 million.

And I almost read it. Instead, I read a review by Tom Smith, the senior study director of the National Opinion Research Center at the University of Chicago.

Smith's review rips the book to shreds. Instead of a significant contribution, he calls it, "a stew of hyperbole, wild gener-alizations, and factoids, based on poorly documented and questionable data, and simplistic and bumbling analysis." His review of their methods and analysis is full of terms like "abandons," "without foundation," "problematic," "ignores," "vague," "central conceit," "cryptically," "vacuous," and my personal favorite, "may have induced frivolousness."

Essentially, we have a microcosm of why it is in fact OK to blame villainous JP for the ills of publishing, entertainment, literacy, and therefore point a literary finger at him—despite his immense success and philanthropic efforts and Read-KiddoRead.com—because time and again, instead of giving us something real, something of value and substance along the lines of *The Thomas Berryman Number*, he chooses what is popular and what sells. With *The Day America Told the Truth,* he missed an opportunity to take on some serious and powerful issues, and instead went for the sensational and eye-catching. Tom Smith puts it this way, "Many personal matters—from sexual practice to drug use—are difficult to measure reliably, but investigators have increasingly improved their measurement of such sensitive attitudes and activities. To this important, ongoing effort, *The Day America Told the Truth* contributes essentially nothing."

$$c = 300 \text{ million readers}$$

The typical American spends more than $2,000 a year to satisfy their craving for entertainment. Two grand to stave off boredom, relax, escape, laugh, sing, dance, be captivated, enthralled, engrossed, amused, titillated, cheered up, inspired, transported, and just plain get away from ourselves. An article in *Business Wire* on "The Luxury of Leisure" lists the following benefits of entertainment: expands the mind through ideas, reduces boredom and stress, expresses different aspects of personality, fantasy fulfillment, self-expression, and enhancement to the quality of life.

This $2,000 a year is also books: hardcovers, paperbacks, and now e-books. For the past thirty years, the wallets of

300 million people and JP have met at the intersection of self-actualization.

Are these 300 million "selecting what they see as good?" Are they making up their own minds? Or is their $29.99 purchase of a JP hardcover being conjured by a master marketer, an insidious villain on a spree through American wallets, that only the intrepid Alex Cross can stop?

One critic put a JP bristler this way: "He is a marketing genius who has cynically maneuvered his way to best-sellerdom by writing remedial novels that pander to the public's basic instincts."

According to JP, his books say, "Read me, enjoy me, have fun. This isn't *Moby Dick*."

Which leads to important questions: Are certain books elitist? What is elitism? Is it bad?

The New Zealand author Eleanor Catton responded to these very questions when a reader accused her of being elitist for using the word "crepuscular." Here is a portion of her reply:

> Elitism is a standard of discernment that seeks to exclude everything (or everyone) perceived to fall short of that standard.
>
> But literature simply cannot be. All a starred review amounts to is an expression of brand loyalty, an assertion of personal preference for one brand of literature above another. It is as hopelessly beside the point as giving four stars to your mother, three stars to your childhood, or two stars to your cat.

In 2013, JP used an entire page in the New York Times to bring our attention to the health (or lack thereof) of our literature. JP expressed his concern like this:

Who will save our books?
Our bookstores?
Our libraries?
If there are no bookstores, no libraries, no serious publishers with passionate, dedicated, idealistic editors, what will happen to our literature? Who will discover and mentor new writers? Who will publish our important books? What will happen if there are no more books like these?

Then he listed forty really good books and points out at the bottom that our federal and state governments aren't really doing anything about the issue.

And here we are with the central JP paradox: The collateral damage of his relentless marketing is that he squeezes out other authors who might write the books that his ad calls for. He promotes his books (on kidnapping, rape, etc.) as books for everyone to enjoy, while the literature he calls for and he himself consumes is concurrently a critically endangered species to rescue and an example of obtuse elitism to ridicule.

He isn't writing for the readers of literary fiction, whom he considers "holier than thou." He knows them because he was one of them, long ago, reading late into the night at the ward. "I was a snob," he says. Then he came down from these lofty pages and found commercial fiction, the fiction for all.

• • •

Clearly though, JP isn't all villainous savvy market manipulator—which makes him a more complex antagonist for this essay. In addition to fighting for his publishing house, he also fights for reading and kids. His website ReadKiddoRead.

com helps parents find books for their kids. He donates innumerable books to schools. You could call his own books a national disgrace, say that he is peddling assembly-line cookie-cutter schlock, but he could look back at you and say, "What have you done? Have you written any best sellers? I didn't think so. And because of me, people are at least reading." And really, what can you say back?

300 million people buying JP books is worthy of examination, and will prove to have some adverse effects, but it is not the calamity that is illiteracy in America, where one in four children in America grows up without learning to read, where two-thirds of students who cannot read proficiently by the end of fourth grade will end up in jail or on welfare, or where 32 million adults—14% of the population—can't read. It's not just an American problem. According to UNICEF, 1 billion people entered the twenty-first century unable to read a book or sign their names; two-thirds of these were women.

Without literacy, a person is looking at life below the poverty line: welfare, jail, unwanted pregnancies, drugs, no internet access, no participation in civic life, burdensome costs to the healthcare and criminal justice systems, and contributing to these depressing statistics. Any kid growing up in America without reading a good book is a kid too many.

For combatting this tragedy, JP is to be commended.

Now, back to why it's also OK to dislike or even despise what JP and his smug expression have become. Because books are like the food we feed our minds. It's one thing to be starving to death. Eating only ketchup, however, is another thing entirely.

$$a = c$$
NYPD RED 2 = 300 million people

I went to the library and checked out five JP books in three different genres, not as a struggling freelance writer writing an essay on JP, but as a reader—number 300,000,001.

I wanted to put *NYPD RED 2* aside and be objective, to give JP a fair shake and read with an open mind. Was he as Stephen King said, "a terrible writer?" Or was he a master storyteller who also happens to be a marketing whiz? Does he really have a "golden gut" for plotting instincts? Do I want to "lean in" to his stories? Where's the fun?

• • •

Timing is everything in life and JP's success is no exception. To understand how books like *NYPD RED 4* debut as #1 on the *USA Today* B.S. list, one has to step back from all the page turning to see the big picture, the forest that is the publishing business.

Some perspective comes from a 2010 JP article in the *New York Times* by J. Mahler. It goes something like this: In the 1980's, just as JP is stumbling upon his lean style of short sentences and chapters, "a wave of consolidation sweeps through the industry." Barnes & Noble and Borders start elbowing out independent bookstores, and the emphasis is on BLOCKBUSTER hardcovers.

In the '90s, these top-selling hard-cover BLOCKBUSTER books give Barnes & Noble and Borders the added leverage to demand discounts from publishers and charge hefty sums for store placement. (Confession: This had never occurred to me.)

One consequence of all the consolidation is that publishers are less inclined to take risks on new authors and undiscovered talent. With the "hefty sums" they have to pay for a spot near the bookstore's entrance, they better be darn sure that the books they put there sell. And so, with shifting economics and the BLOCKBUSTER hardcover getting bigger and bigger, along comes a spider named JP.

Before he crept onto the national scene, there were definitely blockbusters by authors like Mario Puzo, James Michener, and Danielle Steele. But for the first time, publishers start to embrace the template of mass-marketing fiction writers who become their own brands with aggressive promotion, sharper packaging, and slick TV ads. JP becomes recognized within the thriller genre like Skippy in the grocery store—you know what you are getting.

And this is where JP's marketing background and savvy come in. His Alex Cross books have a series-unifying jacket style, with big bold type, colorful lettering, and nursery rhyme titles like *Pop Goes the Weasel, Four Blind Mice,* and *Roses Are Red.*

Publishing books is an "inherently conservative" business, but now with raised stakes it becomes even tighter. An increasingly smaller group of writers dominate national B.S. lists. Placement on the B.S. list gets you placement at the bookstore, the cycle is reinforced and you have BLOCKBUSTERS bigger than the blockbusters of the '70s and '80s.

JP was the perfect writer for this period. This is how he transformed Little, Brown. While the publishing industry around them was in freefall, they were churning out BLOCK-BUSTERS not just from JP, but from Michael Connelly, Stephenie Meyer (Twilight), Malcolm Gladwell, and one of my personal favorites/heroes David Sedaris.

Now, with this context, the **300 million** is making more sense. Just when I thought I could head down to Florida and JP's couch, I peered into a dark and confusing chasm, a 2014 article in the *New Yorker* by George Packer entitled, "Cheap Words." I had to consider the impact of Amazon and e-books on JP and the publishing industry.

It's a rabbit hole, but essentially the dominoes go down something like this: consolidation in publishing and retail —> less risk on new authors —> focus on BLOCKBUSTERS —> Amazon —> fewer professional book reviewers —> fewer knowledgeable booksellers —> self-publishing becomes easier —>more writers —> less talent —> lower and lower prices —> readers conditioned to think books are of minimal value like a 99-cent widget —> too many unfamiliar choices —> *NYPD RED 2* = 400 million books sold

Now the 400 million makes sense. And JP doesn't seem like such a bad, manipulative guy. More of a right place, right time, right skills kind of thing. Still, it's an astonishing accomplishment.

And while I can't quite imagine that many people, much less that many people *reading*, all along I have been able to picture JP's comfortable living room in his Palm Beach home. For some reason, in all the interviews, his wife serves the journalists cookies and this makes it into the story. I can picture this.

In my imagination, I see him welcoming two young writers who have come seeking advice. One of them, let's say her name is Ann Author, is an accomplished author in my head. Let's say she has an M.F.A. in creative writing, some prestigious publishing credentials in literary magazines, and one novel that sold 8,000 copies. But she can't get anyone to publish her second or third novels and she comes to JP at her wit's end.

Let's say the other is named William Writer, and maybe he's not so young anymore. When he came of age, like JP, he read voraciously. But unlike JP, William Writer did not focus as much on stories and became increasingly curious about words and sentences. His undergraduate journalism papers contained sentences like, "Minister administer your eulogy. We have gathered here today," which drew praise from the well-compensated professors. But in the end, how far can well-crafted sentences take you? As most journalism students from the early 2000's can tell you, the answer is: the nearest restaurant hiring servers.

So after college William Writer started serving and stopped writing. Fifteen years later he woke up one morning before dawn and realized he had one great story to tell from his youth, a profoundly American tragedy. He wrote it with sparkly syntax and a bittersweet sense of irony. Like F. Scott Fitzgerald, William had one great novel in him. Now it is two years later and he's twenty pages from completing it. But he has no clue how to navigate the waters of the publishing industry.

Ann and William are sitting there, nibbling cookies, when JP comes in from his morning round of golf. He thanks them for coming and is happy to speak with them. He sips his iced tea and tells them the same things he told a student who posted online about taking JP's master's online writing class. This writer entered with "skepticism or the anticipation of great comedy material, but exited with respect and even affection."

What changed? JP doled out "good solid common sense and genuinely valuable wisdom."

And that's what JP tells Ann and William: that it's not writing but *storytelling*. It's not the story but the telling, as Jack London said. Dialogue needs to be wittier, tighter, more filled with dramatic tension and suspense. Real-life dialogue is tedious. Readers can sense the inauthentic. Spend more time outlining. Make it an experience. Try to be there. Think about your readers and what they want: are they leaning into your story or just nodding along? Make it so the reader has an insatiable need to know what happens. Keep 'em off balance. Write with confidence. And then he says to William, in particular, "When you finish your novel, write another one."

In my imagination, Ann the diligent worker who leaves no stone unturned is recording the conversation AND taking notes. William, who has read some of JP's work, is less enthusiastic. And as the amicable conversation winds down and the two struggling writers stand to leave, I see JP smile warmly at Ann, a smile of encouragement and empathy. A smile that says, "I know how you feel," and "Hang in there, kid," and, maybe even for one tantalizing moment it says, "Who knows, maybe I'll send you an outline one of these days and we can work together—I like the cut of your jib."

Then, for the briefest of moments, there is something of a glare at William. It passes so quickly that no one can say for sure that it happened, but in that flashing moment William glimpses the ruthlessly ambitious advertising shark. The writer who bristles at criticism like "airport author." The person who opened his twentieth anniversary Little, Brown celebration speech with "I'm sorry my good friend Stephen King couldn't be here. It must be bingo night in Bangor." The author who said to the co-president of James Patterson Entertainment, "I'm sorry, Bill, did you recently write an international bestseller that I'm not aware of?" The multi-millionaire who's releasing more than fifteen books this year and is "more motivated than ever." William perceives that behind JP's smile to Ann is also his arrogant attitude toward the literary community in general that says, "Sorry boys!" (All tallies on the Villain column.)

And for an equally brief moment, while Ann Author babbles on about how good the cookies were, William Writer recoils as if he has just looked The Bad Guy in the eye.

• • •

I've read three of the five JP books I checked out from the library. I'm starting to feel a bit like Morgan Spurlock in the 2004 documentary *Super Size Me*, in which the director eats nothing but McDonalds for a month.

The comparison pops into my mind one night as I'm wrestling with my final verdict on JP and his contradictions. Any ire over the state of books and reading in our country directed at JP seems misguided, but is it? There are the contradictions alongside the reality that his books have a certain common sense and wisdom regarding what readers want, how to keep the plot moving, instilling curiosity, and just plain old telling a good story.

But there is something profoundly evasive about it all, something that keeps me working at the equations, something that still doesn't quite add up. One night, as I flipped through the pages of my pretend journalist notebook, I stumbled upon a quote and the knot came loose. Everything fell into place, and I realized that I was doing to my mind what Morgan Spurlock did to his body.

JP said that he is not interested in the readers of literary fiction and views the crowd as a "holier than thou" group. And then he said it.

"I like the notion of being ketchup. It's sweet. It's bitter. It's umami. And satisfies a lot of people. I don't want to write tofu."

JP is ketchup. He is the fast food of books. There is nothing wrong with eating it now and again, like when you are stuck in an airport and there are no other options available. And it's OK if kids eat it, because it's available and affordable and better than not eating.

But when the product is addictive and harmful, lurking

underneath the 400 million books is a problem. Like excess alcohol or tobacco or fast food. Or a truck driver saying, "I've listened to every one of your books on tape and I'm not sure what I would do without you."

Maybe I'm part of the holier than thou group, though I really tried to read his books as reader 300,000,001. I sit in rush hour traffic every day. I don't want to go through life numb. I want to feel more. Yet, when it comes to JP, I find his books to be the antithesis of feeling—his books by their nature repudiate depth. The quickly turning pages offer sex and violence and cunning and twists and suspense, and at times I really try to lean in, to feel the story like the characters do, but I don't really feel for Alex Cross, and 111 chapters into one of his books I don't know why the psychopath is full of rage.

I don't think it's me, even if I am in the holier than thou group. But what do the thousands of *NYPD RED* readers feel? Instead of feeling, they get diversion in the name of entertainment. There's a point when the diversion becomes something more, something insidious and harmful, like an addiction to escape itself. Like cracking open JP instead of digging into real life and relationships and problems and work. Avoid it all and choose three-page chapters without too much detail or depth getting in the way.

JP is not to blame, though. And he knows it. JP was in the right place at the right time. But all of it is bigger than him, even though he's a juggernaut and an easy target for jealousy or ire. It's easy to have disdain for him if you're a fledgling writer like me, because of all his success and the spots he takes up on the B.S. list and how hard it is to get into publishing in general. But really any energy aimed at JP is wasted. It's like blaming Roger Goodell for the ills of the NFL. And while it's valid and instructive to discuss the decisions writers face in literature versus what sells and whether to use "crepuscular" or "twilight," here is where I feel the balance ultimately tips away from Hero and over to Villain.

I have no problem with his commercial success or style or technique or subject matter. The tipping point is a quote from an article in the *Telegraph*: "JP continues to be a voracious reader and every once in a while he'll read a book and think, 'I'd wish I'd written that,' or 'I wish I could be that kind of stylist.' He could do it, he says, but he has no interest in trying."

And that's the real head-scratcher. Why not? Is it because it would be hard? Because he might fail? Because it might be his best book but his worst-selling? Is it too difficult to halt the runaway machine that's churning out these books? Too many commitments to co-writers? Would his publishers and staff not be on board with him going back to the award-winning style of *The Thomas Berryman Number*?

Here is what I would say to JP on his couch: Instead of taking out an ad in the *New York Times* about how there's no one around to help writers produce great fiction, how about using your resources and time and energy to do it yourself? How about taking advantage of your loyal fan base and prominent placement in bookstores and on Amazon to raise the bar of American fiction—just a little, for one book?

But I already know the answer. It wouldn't fit with his brand: sweet, reliable ketchup. And tofu might be good for you, but most people don't know how to cook it.

THE QUINTESSENTIAL PEARL
JAM ALBUM FOR ALIENS

NOTE TO READER: In addition to alien life forms, this essay is targeted at the millions of die-hard Pearl Jam fans out there. You've been warned.

In December of 1965, the first musical performance in space (known to humans, at least) occurred when astronauts on Gemini 6 smuggled a Hohner Little Lady harmonica and a handful of small bells aboard and performed "Jingle Bells" for the crew of Gemini 7 as they completed the first rendezvous between two spacecraft, on their way to the moon. It was a gag.

Then in 1978, cosmonaut Aleksandr I. Ivanchenko strummed an acoustic six string on a Soviet space station (presumably a Russian ditty, but let's not rule out "Free Bird"). Ever since, music has provided psychological support for humans in orbit. Guitars, flutes, keyboards, saxophones, bagpipes, drums (upside down garbage pail), DJ software, and a didgeridoo (Australian aboriginal wind instrument fashioned, in this case, with a vacuum cleaner hose) have all been played in orbit aboard various spacecraft (most notably the ISS).

The Falcon Heavy test flight to Mars, launched on February 6, 2018, included a Tesla Roadster on board blasting David Bowie's "Space Oddity." The song is playing on an endless loop that will continue for the duration of the billion-year orbit.

The rocket contains a 5D laser optical storage device able to withstand the harsh conditions of space. It looks like a CD and contains Isaac Asimov's Foundation book series. If we humans really do want to share some of our culture and experience with an alien life form (considering the psychological benefits of music in space), the next rocket should probably contain a little music, something like. . .

For the purpose of this essay, I will use the definition of "quintessential" from freedictionary.com: the "most typically representative of a quality, state, etc.; perfect." There are other meanings from other dictionaries. For example: the pure and essential essence of something, e.g. the quintessential Jewish delicatessen—which would be a good fit if I ever write an essay on Reuben sandwiches (on my list!). For *this* endeavor, however, I'm using the definition that would apply to the following task: creating a Pearl Jam album to send to aliens from another planet.

To run this particular gauntlet, I will choose one song from each of their eleven studio albums, plus some appropriation from the rest of their vast musical catalog and compilations. I will stay true to the original track listing. For example, only an opening song of an album can be used for track 1, an album's second song for track 2, etc. There are various reasons for doing this, but mainly I want to make it like solving a puzzle.

As a die-hard PJ fan, I will try to avoid my own personal bias and taste. And while my theme might be tongue-in-cheek, I hope to show that Pearl Jam, like all great rock 'n' roll bands, are in the business of saving the planet, one human being at a time.

SIDE 1 TRACK 1

The initial temptation is to begin with "Once." In some ways, it might even be a no-brainer. What better way to introduce an alien civilization to a rock band than to begin with the first song on their first album? Yet Pearl Jam, like their mentors the Who, are a live band first and foremost, that then try to duplicate live performances on their albums. Therefore, it makes sense for the album to represent the live experience, since PJ will probably not play in space any time soon (though they might play there before China).

Pearl Jam typically opens with a slow song, sort of a warm-up. This leaves two options: "Can't Keep" from *Riot Act* and "Sometimes" from *No Code*. It's essentially a toss-up, which forces me to examine the other songs from each of these albums for a track that I might want to keep available. *No Code* marked an important new path for the band musically, showing an experimental side not really concerned with commercial success or mass appeal. So it's tempting to save a tune like "Who You Are" or "I'm Open" for later, in the interest of offering a different flavor on the alien's plate. But on further review, *Riot Act* loses (or wins, depending on your perspective) the opening track battle on the basis of its distinction as the longest Pearl Jam album with fifteen tracks (which will come in handy later).

The opening song is "Sometimes" from *No Code*.

SIDE 1 TRACK 2

The second song of many Pearl Jam shows follows the warm-up like an uppercut follows a jab. There is no shortage of second tunes on their albums that do just this. Some more than others, but basically every second song on every album, except "Faithful" on *Yield,* is an up-tempo, hard rocker.

What is initially an easy, take-your-pick decision becomes complex when considering the daunting task of my Sudoku-style format. I have to take into account songs that won't be available and weigh them in the balance. Hence (that's right, I just used the word "hence" in an essay about PJ), the prudent approach here is to leave ALL of the albums on the table and veer into their other studio releases. The second song on the soundtrack for the Cameron Crowe movie *Singles,* entitled "Breath," would work well for the purpose of taking an aggressive, uplifting rock 'n' roll swing at everything that might be depressing a spaceship full of aliens. After all, space probably gets lonely.

The second song is "Breath" from the *Singles* soundtrack.

SIDE 1 TRACK 3

The third song is obvious: "Alive" from the album *Ten.* If there is a casual fan at a Pearl Jam concert who is drunk and irritated that Eddie Vedder is discussing politics for going on five minutes, that fan will be equally elated singing along to the chorus, "Ohhhhhhhhhhhh ahhhhhhyyyyyyeeeeeeeee, aaaaaaaaahhhhh ahhhhhhhhh ahhhhmmmm still alive, yeeeeeeaaaaahhhhhh!"

Now, as all die-hard fans know, Vedder's lyrics are autobiographical, about a son finding out that who he thought was his real father is actually his stepdad, and that his real father is dead. This is not hard to grasp from the song's first listen. Yet until this essay, even after many, many listens, I never took the second, completely messed up, and dark turn into the song's other meaning: the incestuous relationship with the mother. The son has become a spitting *and* desirable image of the mother's one true love. While the song *is* autobiographical, the second verse, the dark turn, is just good old-fashioned storytelling.

Vedder revealed that the "she" in the second verse was the mother, and "the look" he referred to was not the look on her face. "The look is between her *legs*. Where do you go with *that*? That's where you came from."

Now the aliens might be a tad perplexed here, but they also would be pleased to know that the tune has literally taken on a new meaning thanks to the audience interpreting the song as inspirational. The song is no longer a burden but a blessing. And the aliens will find the chorus to be equally inspiring, followed by Mike McCready's solo that, if they are wearing socks (which they might be because it's cold in space), would get knocked off.

INSERT SOUND EFFECT HERE—SOMETHING SIMILAR TO THE DAILY DOUBLE ON JEOPARDY! SOUND (BUT NOT TOO SIMILAR. COPYRIGHT LAWS, Y'ALL)

It's time for our first hidden track! That's right. For three reasons: 1) I can't compile a rock album without also including the novelty of a hidden track. 2) *Gigaton* wasn't written or even rumored about, much less released when I first patted myself on the back upon completion of this essay, back in 2015. (The lack of prior publication is a sore subject I won't go into. 3) Rather than move everything around, it's much easier to create a hidden track and cram the song wherever I want.

SIDE 1 TRACK 3B (HIDDEN)

Here is my first real temptation for personal bias. The song "River Cross" is my favorite track on the new album. The song struck me like a bolt of lightning. As a wannabe writer whose

number of ignored or rejected queries was approaching something of a threshold, the phrase "published author" started to
feel like that shore, that other side that I nearly reached (i.e. I've
had manuscripts requested by agents at reputable houses, the
New Yorker personally rejected one of my pieces with "despite
the evident merit"), but then the river *turned and widened*.
Also, the closing song of *Gigaton* is the timeliest song for the
pandemic, as evidenced by Vedder performing "River Cross"
for Global Citizen's "Together at Home" broadcasted show
curated by Lady Gaga.

However, the purpose of this essay/album is not bound by
any period or time or sense of chronology. The objective is
QPJ (Quintessential Pearl Jam). To this purpose, the third
track, "Dance of the Clairvoyants" is the most QPJ because of
its experimental nature and evidence of musical exploration.
I could pick "Superblood Wolfmoon" or "Seven O'Clock" or
any handful of tunes that would get some alien blood (if they
have blood; if not, fluids anyway) pumping. Here is what Jeff
Ament said about the song: "'Dance' was a perfect storm of
experimentation and real collaboration, mixing up the instru-
mentation and building a great song…Did I mention…that
Stone is playing bass on this one? We›ve opened some new
doors creatively and that›s exciting."

So track 3 is "Alive" from *Ten* followed by a short silence and
then "Dance of the Clairvoyants" from *Gigaton*.

SIDE 1 TRACK 4

Here it is tempting to pick the next track 4 that is available, "glorified g" from *Vs*. Notably, this song is anti-gun and anti-violence,
and since "Jeremy" is already lost, what better way to make up
for it than to choose the funky riff of "glorified g."

But of course, I have to look ahead, and I quickly see some track 4 heavy-hitters that I have to think long and hard about keeping off the list. I can see some Pearl Jam fan confronting me at a show years from now—and they are stone-sober mind you—for leaving off "Light Years." Like right up in my grill. And then there's "Given to Fly", which is a QPJ ode to freedom and surfing, which I could equally foresee as a confrontation-worthy omission.

Looking ahead to what I will need down the line, I can see I'm up the proverbial creek on this one. Time to buckle down and make some hard choices. This selection is critical in setting up later options. There's no going back. Therefore, with a bit of trepidation for future run-ins with disgruntled PJ fans, I will make "Light Years" from *Binaural* my selection.

Here's why: when I picture an alien hearing the song for the first time, for some reason I see Kang and Kodos Johnson from *The Simpsons*. I imagine that they quickly grasp that the song is about loss. Further, I envision a situation years later, after many space voyages, where, say Kodos, perhaps inspired by the QPJA, has become a touring musician and is playing to a packed stadium usually reserved for alien sports. Allow me the liberty to imagine that comedic characters are not immune to tragedy: at the same time, Kang lies in an alien hospital bed with a particularly aggressive form of alien brain cancer, like glioblastoma. Kodos, on stage at the alien stadium, thinks back fondly to their years of space travel and wants to dedicate a song to Kang. He might choose "Light Years" (much like Pearl jam dedicated the tune to singer Gordon Downie at a 2016 Wrigley Field show, mindful that just north of the border, the Tragically Hip was performing the final show of their farewell tour in Ontario). I can picture Kodos, his large cyclops eye welling up with tears, as he belts out the verse, "your life made of stars."

Now, if you still have the urge to confront me with facial proximity, know that this decision did not come lightly. Shoot, a pun. Quick, on to track 5!

SIDE 1 TRACK 5

The five slot on Pearl Jam albums is full of great tunes, like the already forsaken "Black," "Smile," and "Nothing as It Seems." There's also "Wishlist", "Lightning Bolt" to consider, and a song that I just recently heard Willie Nelson cover with one of his sons, "Just Breathe."

Again, I have to weigh my options carefully and scrutinize each available song/album for overall PJ quintessential-ness.

Really, this one is pretty easy. For die-hard fans, there are songs that reach another level, a visceral deepness that connects with the seat of imagination, passion, will, and drive. The song "Just Breathe" from the album *Backspacer* does exactly that.

There are lots of things out there in psychology and self-help and the lot that can basically be summed up as positive thinking and gratitude. Therapists and other professionals argue that just by listing things you are thankful for, you can improve your overall happiness and mental health. "Just Breathe" is about human need. People need basic acceptance, understanding, and love, just as they need oxygen.

While aliens from outer space may or may not have respiratory systems involved in two-way gas exchange, if they are living things with basic needs, they will appreciate this particular addition.

SIDE 1 TRACK 6

Ah, the throw away track. Some may call it an album filler. Some may bristle at the term, or even at the *mere suggestion* of the concept. Still, let's call a duck a duck. Pearl Jam is no stranger to having a song on an album that falls into the category of album filler. It's not something to cringe at or label as necessarily bad or get any hypothetical undergarments into any kind of twist about. In fact, the filler is something of an art form in itself. Look at the Beatles or Pink Floyd.

Vitalogy has—count them—four album fillers (not counting "Satan's Bed"). These songs are all evidence that an album that is QPJ needs a little aside, a little break before resuming with the heavy lifting. For this purpose, I will reach out to Vedder's solo album *Into the Wild* for track 6, "Tuolumne." It's a nice little breather, very relaxing and mellow, something you can close your eyes to and pretend you're staring out at an Alaskan wilderness or, say, swirling clouds on a gaseous planet.

SIDE 1 TRACK 7

Luckily, I planned ahead for this one. There is no way to have a QPJA without "Do the Evolution" from *Yield*. This song, perhaps more than any other, shows the need to have a sampling from each period of their career.

The lyrics shine a light on all the ironic, hypocritical idiots out there working in the name of progress. Me too, probably. We're so advanced, wearing pants and plundering the planet. We've evolved so far as a human race, well beyond the "ignorant Indians," but we still murder, go to war, pollute, and are powerless in our gas-guzzling trucks to stop the fire of greed consuming our planet.

Or something like that.

Either way, this is a great tune to hear at a concert or on a ride home from work, so I presume it works for intergalactic travel as well. A must for a QPJA.

SIDE 1 TRACK 8

Side One ends with Pearl Jam's best driving song, "Rearview-mirror" from *Vs.* ("MFC" is second, but it's not close.) In fact, I would argue that "rvm" belongs on a list of all-time best driving songs. Yet my Google search for said lists returned nary a "rvm" on nary a list. To show my disappointment, I've decided to use the word nary in one more sentence. Then nary a murmur shall I make.

Pearl Jam demonstrates their high esteem for "rvm" by busting it out regularly towards the end of shows or to close out a set.

Anyway, the alien spaceships probably don't have rearview mirrors, and they probably go pretty darn fast anyway to get to our galaxy within whatever their lifespans are, but once they hear "rvm" it's safe to assume they might drive/fly/zoom through space just a little faster.

This concludes SIDE ONE. I trust that the Arch Mission Foundation, a nonprofit designed to preserve human heritage forever, (the same people who made the 5D laser optical storage device with Asimov's books on the Falcon Flight to Mars) will figure out a way to protect vinyl in space— or at least devise something that preserves the crackle and hiss.

SIDE 2 TRACK 9

The remaining four Pearl Jam albums provide some interesting options for Track 9. Maybe an argument could be made for these tunes, but instead, I'm going to veer way off the beaten path. For one thing, it's important to show some of the amazing collaborations Pearl Jam has done in their career.

Side Two starts out with the ninth track off *Mirror Ball*, an album that features the members of Pearl Jam sans Eddie Vedder (mostly), with Neil Young taking the lead. Neil Young later described this album as "a big smoldering mass of sound."

While "Throw Your Hatred Down" might not be as QPJ as, say, "Peace And Love," (which does feature a verse by Vedder), my selection is a great tune—raw, simple, and melodic like the rest of the album. Plus it features a quintessential PJ theme: anti-violence and love conquering hate.

INSERT SOUND EFFECT HERE—SOMETHING SIMILAR TO THE DAILY DOUBLE ON JEOPARDY! SOUND (BUT NOT TOO SIMILAR. COPYRIGHT LAWS, Y'ALL)

SIDE 2 TRACK 9B (HIDDEN)

Here, after a brief silence, I segue right into our second hidden track: track 9 from Temple of the Dog's self-titled (and only) album, which happens to be "Four Walled World." Again, one might object, saying that this isn't a very QPJ song, and that I should abandon this bizarre Sudoku business and choose the best (read: most popular) song, in this instance "Hunger Strike." But I would argue that my approach is QPJ, traveling into the obscure and rare. Plus, now the QPJA features a hidden track that has Chris Cornell singing, which is sure to raise some alien eyebrows, or whatever they have evolved above their eyes that helps express emotion, hair-based or otherwise.

SIDE 2 TRACK 10

Not to say that QPJ sets out to be intentionally rare or obscure. QPJ is also mainstream, popular, even sing-songy campfire music. Track 10 is a good illustration of this.

The song, "Last Kiss," conveniently appears as track 10 on *Lost Dogs* Disc 2. This is a cover of a song originally written by Wayne Cochran in 1961. The song bounced around a little before gaining more notoriety from J. Frank Wilson & the Cavaliers in 1964. With PJ, the song eventually reached #2 on the Billboard Hot 100, the highest position of any Pearl Jam song.

Since space travel is long and lonely, an alien might pass some time glancing through the QPJA liner notes. Here I go again with the alien assumptions: To achieve the scientific prowess required to access the album, the life form is probably loaded in the intelligence domain. So let's say this creature, flipping through the liner notes and lyrics, while listening to the album, does pretty well cracking the code of our alphabet and putting together sounds and words. And after reading about "Last Kiss," he/she/they stumble on this realization: a gifted band like Pearl Jam can spend hours and hours rehearsing and writing and rewriting and recording scores of songs, or they can go into a used record store, fall in love with a song, record a cover of it at a sound check, release it as holiday single, and that is the song that sells the most copies of their entire catalog. Go figure.

SIDE 2 TRACK 11

I am, in my own eyes, a songwriter. The less I say about my own songwriting here the better, but I bring it up because, as someone who has put a pen to paper in the act of writing a song, I can appreciate perhaps just a shade more than the average musical consumer who has never written a song what it must feel like to play several notes and have a stadium full of people immediately cheer in recognition and anticipation.

That is what happens when Vedder plays the broken D chord that introduces the QPJ song "Better Man" live. This is a song that people pay money to hear. If people hear this song at a concert, they go home happy, like a crowd of people leaving a football arena after the home team has won. Conversely, a casual fan might be walking down the ramp and say something like, "That was a good show, but they didn't play 'Better Man.'"

The lyrics describe the struggle to end an abusive relationship and, in QPJ fashion, has also become about catharsis—another QPJ trait. (In fact, it might be the second most cathartic PJ song, right behind "Release.") All of us carry around pain in the form of memories, situations and problems that are unresolved. *Vitalogy's* "Better Man" takes that pain and smashes it, exposes it, triumphs over it, which is not just what QPJ is about—it's the essence of rock 'n' roll.

SIDE 2 TRACK 12

We're getting down to the nitty-gritty. It's time to turn to the band's second most recent album, *Lightning Bolt*. While the most QPJ song on the album is "Sirens," that doesn't fit into the puzzle as it's not the twelfth track. I've made my bed, as the saying goes. So, instead I will select the closing track, "Future Days." This is where I come close to violating my oath not to include personal likes and favorites. To avoid this unseemly awkwardness, I will share the tale of a recent morning when a Pearl Jam fan I know, who will go by the name Listener X, happened to be driving to work and suddenly became very tired of the sports radio show he was listening to. Worn thin by this (and more), X changed the satellite radio station and happened to catch the very beginning of "Future Days," a song X had not *really* listened to until this very moment. To put it simply, the song gave X the needed boost, the hold on the proverbial boot strap, to pull up and out of his weary morning funk and face the day, to believe that the day itself, the drive and the job and the red lights and all the little things X would do/endure/face on his daily odysseys counted toward something. Something that matters. (Not to get all sentimental but, to this day, when X sees the morning sun on these specific pine trees on this particular stretch of road, sometimes X is reminded of this tune and gets the chills thinking of his daughters.) What could be more QPJ than that?

SIDE 2 TRACK 13

There are many reasons to include "Inside Job" from Pearl Jam's self-titled album (aka the "Avocado album") on a QPJA. For one thing, the song shows the band's versatility in song writing because Mike McCready wrote the music and words. Also, it includes Boom Gaspar on keyboards, something probably not featured enough on this album. The song hits on a number of QPJ themes and ideas, most saliently the notion of controlling your own thoughts and attitudes, the "I am mine" (i.e. "I won't back down") despite what the world will throw at you in the form of sorrow, loss, disease, and despair. Finally, right towards the end of the song, with the final chorus and YEEEEEAAAAAAHHHHHS of EV, the entire band shifts into another gear. Few bands have this extra gear, but it is on display at the end of "Inside Job." McCready basically goes ballistic on his solo, Vedder is howling, and the whole band is right there, backing it all up. The aliens are going to be psyched.

SIDE 2 TRACK 14

For track 14, I will draw from the last of my available Pearl Jam studio releases, *Riot Act*. The song, aptly named "Arc," is one minute, five seconds, and nine loops of a wordless vocal that pays tribute to the nine people killed in a crowd surge at the Roskilde Festival in Copenhagen, Denmark, on June 30th, 2000. Said EV, "No words, because there's no words for what that situation was. It's kind of like a prayer."

Thus emerges another quality to PJ: dealing with things head-on, whether it is an unfathomable tragedy, a political issue, a relationship, or merely a confrontation with one's self and all of its, for lack of a better psychological term, BS. There's nothing passive about the approach— something the aliens are sure to grasp. It's not pathological but the antithesis: it's the road to health and wellness, mental and physical.

SIDE 2 TRACK 15

To make it to the end, and maybe for a small dose of leniency, track 15 is basically like my Free Space. I'm going to take a live performance of the Neil Young classic, "Rockin' in the Free World." Really any version would do, but since it is *my* free space, I will take a version I used to have on a cassette tape from the Pinkpop festival in Landgraaf, Netherlands, in June of 1992. The song, which closes out their rainy set at the festival, begins with a medley featuring the last verse of a song called "Suggestion" by Fugazi, followed by the first verse of the Talking Heads song "Pulled Up," and then what I believe to be a brief improvisational song called the "The First Time," just drums and EV, slightly building and mounting until the band rips into a raw "RITFW," igniting the entire festival of muddied thousands into a furious frenzy. I'll have to include a note for the aliens to go on autopilot for this one with a definition of the terms: "moshing" and "mosh pit."

SIDE 2 TRACK 16

The only way to end the QPJA album is the same way PJ closes many of their concerts: with "Yellow Ledbetter" (which, ahem, also happens to be track 16 on *Lost Dogs* Disc 1).

This is a song about saying good-bye. As McCready said, it has become like a bookend for over three hundred live shows. There's a reason the producers of *Friends* chose to play it as Rachel is about to board a plane to France in the last episode.

The song embodies this feeling of departure, of all the times when life requires you to turn the page, and you can't put it into words, you don't know how to say good-bye or even *if* to say good-bye to people you may never see again, and this is all captured by the Michael Stipe-esque mumbling verses leading up to the climactic, "I don't want to staaaaaaaaaaaA AAAAAAaaaaaaaaayyyy."

Because it's not just the negative, but more the whole range of Leaving Emotions. Because sometimes, hearing the song, it's that you DO want to stay. You want to stay the way you are. Whatever stage that is, be it concert stage or period of life. Young and healthy. In a good job. Happy. Holding young children as a proud parent. In love. Playing music in front of thousands of fans. But life is change. You can't escape it. You have to change: You have to leave things and people and places behind. So even when it's joyful, it's tinged with sadness because soon it's about to be. . . over. The show. The job. The relationship. The period in your life. The QPJA essay. The lights are on. McCready is playing "Little Wing" and then "The

Star-Spangled Banner," and now it really is over. It's time to go.

In conclusion, the collective takeaway after a listen to the Quintessential Pearl Jam Album, in this human being's humble opinion, would be that life is worth living, love is possible, and the Earth is worth keeping/ fighting for. All things any intelligent life form—with tentacles or otherwise—should be able to take away.

TRACK LISTING

SIDE ONE: 1. Sometimes (*No Code)* 2. Breath (*Singles* soundtrack*)* 3. Alive (*Ten)* > Dance of the Clairvoyants (*Gigaton*) 4. Light Years (*Binaural*) 5. Just Breathe (*Backspacer)* 6. Tuolumne (*Into the Wild* soundtrack) 7. Do the Evolution (*Yield) 8.* Rearviewmirror (*Vs.)*

SIDE TWO: 9. Throw Your Hatred Down (*Mirror Ball*) > Four Walled World (*Temple of the Dog*) 10. Last Kiss (*Lost Dogs* Disc 2*)* 11. Better Man (*Vitalogy)* 12. Future Days (*Lightning Bolt)* 13. Inside Job (self-titled album: *Pearl Jam*, aka "the Avocado Album") 14. Arc (*Riot Act*) 15. Rockin' in the Free World (Neil Young cover. . .probably track 15 on some live album?) 16. Yellow Ledbetter (*Lost Dogs* Disc 1*)*

WITH OR WITHOUT YOU
The Tiers of Fantasy Sports Addiction

With or without you
With or without you
I can't live with or without you

—U2

It started rather innocuously, like most addictions. Donovan McNabb threw four tuddies against the Rams in week 1 of the 2008 NFL season. Later that day, I glanced online. I was winning.

Four weeks later, thanks to McNabb, Larry Fitzgerald, Roddy White, and Frank Gore, I was 4-0. Each win was like a little pleasure shot, a small boost to the psyche, a pat on the back. Victory. Dopamine to the brain.

Then, in week 5, now perilously on the edge of an addiction, yet without any awareness, like a child meandering on the edge of a wall overlooking deep, tumultuous water, I pulled Roddy White against the Bears and unconsciously broke one of the Cardinal Sins of Fantasy Sports: never act with your heart.

As a lifelong Bears fan, the move was a combination of arrogance (confidence in the Bears D—Lovie Smith in general and Charles "Peanut" Tillman specifically) and a repudiation of hedging. It was All or None. All meaning the Bears would win, Roddy White would be contained and stifled while on my fantasy bench, the Turnstyles would win, and I would be 5-0, alone on top of the standings.

But what happened in real life was None: Roddy White went off, while sitting on my fantasy bench, to the tune of 9 catches for 112 yards and a tuddy; the Bears blew a gutsy comeback with the Lovie Smith tentative don't-lose strategy of pooch kicking and then prevent defense, allowing a game-winning 48-yard Jason Elam FG as time expired; and the Turnstyles lost to BK is Good for You. I had to swallow my first taste of fantasy defeat, made worse by the knowledge that I, in a sense, had defeated myself.

The addiction, like a hook in a fish's mouth, was set. I had felt the high from winning and the low from losing. And I liked it. I vowed that week to never let my heart interfere again. I would be shrewd and cold-blooded. Then, I moved Roddy White into the WR1 slot, over Larry Fitzgerald, as a gesture of restitution.

• • •

Most people join a fantasy sports league as a way to connect with other people, socialize, and gain a sense of camaraderie. Maybe it's an office, or a neighborhood, or in my case, a group of friends that collectively start a league to ensure contact. Since two-thirds of all fantasy sports players are men, this then becomes a means for communication, something men sorely need.

TYPICAL MALE CONVERSATION:

"Hey bro, what's up?"
"Not much. What's up with you?"
"Nada."
"Cool."
"Cool."

So it's social, fun, a good time. A harmless diversion from the seriousness of life. It's contact and maybe even a small antidote for the big L, Loneliness. There are plenty of studies out there showing that socially isolated people have shorter life spans and are at a higher risk of infections, disease, and depression. Imagine an M.D. prescribing join a fantasy sports league. Maybe it's not that crazy. Like Pete in *Knocked Up.* We just need a little time away, a break in the action, a friend we can talk flex spots with. We all need a little Matsui now and again.

Fantasy sports are prodigiously popular. 56.8 million people—14% of the U.S. population—played in some sort of fantasy sports league in 2015, according to the Fantasy Sports Trade Association. The rise could even be labeled meteoric, as the numbers have grown from one million in 1991, to 15 million in 2003, to 30 million in 2008, 40 million in 2015, and now somewhere around a cool sixty mill who expend limited brain power to come up with a team name, something like "Luck Be a Brady" or "Rubba Chubb Chubb" or "Thielen Groovy." According to surveys, most of these are college-educated people earning more than $75,000. There are roughly forty million fantasy football owners out there. And with daily fantasy sports leagues gaining steam, there's no drop-off in sight.

But what if underneath this pleasant ha-ha, good-clean-fun social exterior lurks something dark, even sinister? What if the entire pursuit—for *millions of people*—which began innocuously, casually, and socially, becomes something of an obsession? To take it a step further, what if it's sort of like a ladder structure, like the kind they make with position players to help you draft, say, TEs? What if there are tiers of fantasy sports addicts?

• • •

Whoa there, cowboy! is probably what you're thinking. Sure, you say, maybe a few nut jobs here and there might take it too seriously, but certainly they are the exception among the millions who play. We can all roll our eyes and be glad that we're not like that, that we don't live in Loserville, in the Pathetic neighborhood of Just Plain Sad Town, eating frozen waffles for dinner in our mom's basement.

But here's the real-life kicker: What if it isn't the occasional loony in his basement? What if there are really thousands or even millions of people out there putting emotional stock in fantasy sports and being followed like a shadow by a borderline addiction? Maybe it's not you, but someone close to you, and this individual spends A LOT of time on this pursuit. And anything you spend time on, you invest in, with your energy and your psyche and your very soul.

Which brings us to very serious terms that will now comprise entire sentences. Addiction. Gambling. Pernicious. Pathological. Screws Up Your Real Life. Yikes.

Fantasy football like crack cocaine? That's a good one. Ha-ha. As you glance at your phone to check a fantasy app, followed by the tongue-in-cheek, "I was just checking my crack." Your little harmless distraction.

Before we get to the Tiers, let's take a peek beneath the surface on this one, just to be sure there's nothing too apt in the comparison. There are, after all, a lot of parallels. For one thing, it has the never-gonna-happen-to-me hallmark. And then, of course, there's what happens in the brain when your man goes off for four tuddies.

• • •

Unlike some data, like the typical spoken words per day for the average man versus the average woman, the science is clear on this one thanks to brain imaging. C2K rips off a 94-yard tuddy and the reward circuit activates. The pleasure center lights up like a pinball game, Ding-Ding-Ding, with a capital D as in the neurotransmitter Dopamine. The same thing you feel when you exercise, eat a good meal, have sex, or just plain do something right.

It feels good, deep in the brain. But the slippery slope in fantasy sports is that now the pathway for an addiction is open, just like when someone gambles, or smokes weed, or tries heroin, or crack cocaine. It's taking a hit. It's getting high.

Internet addictions have yet to make the cut as an official psychological disorder. And whether fantasy sports should be classified as gambling has been debated in New York courts and other places. The Fantasy Sports Trade Association claims (with a straight face) that it is "skill." And then there's the whole can of worms that is insider information and that one guy who got busted. But it's safe to come back from the ledge of all that and say that the pathways and reward system in the brain are the same in fantasy sports as they are in gambling. Inside the brain, all addictions have essentially the same mechanism (to my limited understanding, anyway). The lawyers and psychologists can call it whatever they want.

An interesting phenomenon that scientists have discovered

involving gambling and the brain is that even "near misses" feel good. Almost winning, or coming this close, also releases dopamine. When you combine that with the reality of dopamine and chemical tolerance, you can see how a fun, harmless pastime like fantasy sports, or playing a little blackjack or poker, or betting on the ponies with disposable income can, for some, approach the territory of vice, addiction, harm, or even ruin.

Enter daily sports leagues. This is not so social, or anywhere near the vicinity of camaraderie. This is fantasy and gambling joined at the hip. (Thankfully, it's pretty much outside the scope of this essay.)

One site claims that 80 percent of Americans have gambled at one time or another. Most of this is the harmless Super Bowl pool or NCAA bracket or Friday night game of poker. Yet within this 80 percent is a group of people that have a full-on gambling PROBLEM. An addiction that is problematic and maybe even devastating. Studies vary, but the estimate is that somewhere between 0.2 and 5 percent of gamblers struggle and walk the line of an addiction.

To apply these numbers to the roughly sixty million fantasy sports players in 2022, if we go conservative and say that only 1 percent of all fantasy football gamblers have an addiction, we arrive at six hundred thousand people out there who are basically obsessed and chained like a dog to the ESPN bottom line, their smart phones, and Adam Schefter's tweets. If we instead lean toward the high end, which is entirely reasonable, we end up with 3 million (to quote Ursula from *The Little Mermaid*—I have daughters, OK?) "poor, unfortunate souls." This then becomes the first tier.

TIER ONE

You've got your typical first tier TE's like Mark Andrews and Travis Kelce, and you've got your first-tier addicts. A clear cut above the rest. Rob Gronkowski was the original stand-alone fantasy tight end, so I'll use the term "Gronk-level addict" to refer to this tier of addiction. These are the 0.2 to 5 percent of the people with a PROBLEM, the ones that daily sports leagues cater to with an onslaught of advertising, false promises, and websites like casinos.

Daily fantasy sports, or DFS, have been compared to an alcoholic discovering an entire new street full of bars, really fun bars that are always crowded and have great drink specials. The Tier 1 Gronk-level addict now has a seamless and smooth merge/upgrade/escalation from the season-long slog that his multiple season-long commitments with friends entails. Now there is immediate winning and losing—and immediate, serious money, mostly being lost.

Time is one way to assign the tiers. Gronk-level addicts watch something like sixteen hours of football in a given week during the season. And all of this doesn't count any time spent researching, studying, following Adam Schefter or Matthew Berry, or the countless others who are perpetually offering updates, latest news, or draft prep.

The minimum for most Gronk-level addicts is likely an hour or two of pre-game *Fantasy Football Now* along with regular weekly internet/Twitter research to help set the line up or make a move on the waiver wire.

The maximum here represents a somewhat frightening reality for people who spend ALL OF THEIR time researching, doing analytics, etc. with the very real possibility that these Gronk-like Tier 1 addiction freaks are not (unless they win) getting paid to do so.

Not to mention reading whole entire books on the subject, like neuroscientist Renee Miller's *Cognitive Bias in Fantasy Sports: Is Your Brain Sabotaging Your Team?* or J.J. Zachariason's *The Late Round QB*, a persuasive counter argument to the fantasy dogma that says owners must draft elite QB's to win championships. Try reading that one at a bookstore around eligible ladies and see how many digits you collect.

Tier 1 addicts play fantasy sports year-round with dynasty football teams, not to mention fantasy baseball, basketball, golf, hockey, or what have you. These other sports are like little hits to keep the addiction at bay, until football returns.

It's debatable whether Tier 1 contains the likes of neuroscientist Renee Miller: people who stay up late due to a busy life schedule and thus deprive themselves of much needed REM sleep. Plus there's the hallmark of joining multiple leagues— like Renee's seven—and then of course there's the entirely different beast of daily leagues. I mean, if the addict holds down a good job and their addiction is only harming themselves, i.e. making them feel *at times* sad, lonely, or tired, but not doing any real harm to anyone else. So maybe this is all much ado.

It's also debatable whether or not fantasy experts who are fortunate enough to earn a living (a pretty darn good one for the best in the biz) writing articles or draft day manifestos or advice columns (or, again, whole actual books like Matthew Berry's *A Fantasy Life,* which landed on the *NY Times* B.S. list) belong in Tier 1, because, much like a professional gambler who makes a sustainable living on gambling they could rationally argue that it is not in fact a problem at all. It's an awesome *career.*

Let's be clear: on Tier 1 IT IS A GAMBLING PROBLEM in the sense that it negatively affects other aspects of a person's life. And really, Tier 1 is nothing new or earth-shattering. But what might be very earth-shattering indeed (and the actual point of this essay) is the tier below.

TIER TWO

Tier 2, TE-speaking, is basically a whole lot of everybody else. For example, in the 2017 season, after your Gronk and Kelce, there were ten or twelve TE's who all fall into the category of TE1 (meaning in the top twelve TE's that should be started in standard leagues). This ranges from the third ranking TE, Zach Ertz, to the twelfth ranking, which happened to be Ben Watson. Essentially, there's not much of a difference, statistically between the third ranking and the twelfth (e.g. third-ranked Greg Olsen in 2015 had 1,104 receiving yards and seven tuddies, while twelfth-ranked Delanie Walker had 1,088 yards and six tuddies, respectively. This pattern manifests itself each year, though you could argue Ertz in 2017 was like a Tier 1.5).

Here is what actually may be (relatively) earth-shattering. What if the Tier 2 of Fantasy Player Addictions actually resembled the TE tiers? Take, for example, the lone 24-year-old waiter diagnosed with ADHD who can't get his life on track and sees a psychologist to complain about how he can't seem to do anything worthwhile, and fantasy football—the only thing that makes him feel good—is taking over his life. What if, instead of these cases being crazy outliers, in reality a *significant* percentage of all fantasy sports players are on the cusp and have experienced the harmful effects of an addiction to fantasy sports?

Let's call it 40 percent, which would put it at around 24 million *poor unfortunate souls. In pain! In need!* Remember, these people aren't Gronk-like addicts—that's a whole different level of addiction. But these are people who may, at times, experience some adverse effects like spending too much—whether it's time or money or thought. Maybe it's as simple as checking your phone for an update on your squad when you should be spending time with your kids. Maybe all these little moments that you miss start to add up in your subconscious. Maybe you have thoughts like, "I just won my fantasy league after five months of grinding away on the internet; why do I feel like a loser?"

Because, like a drug, fantasy sports are a MOOD ALTERER. Checking your phone to see that Giancarlo Stanton has gone yard twice and Boom— how you like me now, Big Red Machine? Simultaneously, glancing down to see that Chris Sale isn't starting because of a uniform incident and is facing a team suspension while the two-year-old at your knees that is crying to use the potty or read a book or use the blue crayon not the red crayon how could you even think that I would want the red crayon, or whatever—these cries are just a little bit more caustic or penetrating or irritating because why can't Sale just wear the old unis and go out and fan 12 like normal?

The access is a blessing and a curse. When your guys are in action, and you're in the second tier of addiction, you need to know NOW. It's in your pocket. Life can wait—be it work or family or whatever. You need the drug.

Baseball is 162 games. It's spread out from the end of March to early October. A long and— even for the most enthusiastic—at times tedious march. Football is more intense. It's a four-month roller coaster that crashes and burns or sails to the Promised Land: the Fantasy Playoffs, which, it just so happens, coincides with the holiday season.

Imagine sitting at a family holiday gathering, watching children opening presents, precious memories that are fleeting and the very substance of happiness—all of this while in the next room, the real smack awaits: RedZone coverage of nine 1 p.m. Eastern kickoff match-ups, the screen on but unwatched, the volume set on mute, and you're in the semifinals with five months of soul-invested hours on the line, and all you can think of is, What is happening with My Guys? Was that my opponent's player being carted off the field in Kansas City? Is it too soon to go to the restroom again?

This is the second tier. It's everybody below the hard addicts, which I contend are Gronk-like and rare. How many millions walk this line? How many cross over, back and forth into this wasteland? Or even just stand on the edge and occasionally dip their toe in?

It's the guy who pulls the car over on a family vacation and climbs rocks vainly attempting to get a bar of service on his phone rather than suffer another of fantasy sports' Cardinal Sins: the ignominious vacant roster spot. It's the guy (or gal) who chooses fantasy football over real-life relationships. It's the guy who chooses the real-life relationship but is sullen and withdrawn at the real-life event because he would rather be in his basement with RedZone. It's the person who chooses fantasy over sleep. These are functioning, maybe even highly proficient adults who admit, yeah, there's some negative side effects like being tired, but I'll just grab a Starbucks and power through because missing the playoffs for a third year in a row is not an option. It's more than a hobby for our Tier 2 addicts; it's obsessing, at times mildly but still obsessing: over scores or trades or lineups or fantasy wins and losses.

For Tier 1 addicts, it consumes, eats away. It's always happening and within reach. For Tier 2, it becomes, somehow, *sustainable*. It's on the verge of being full-blown but never goes off the deep end. It flares up, it Dr-Jekyll-and-Mr-Hydes.

There's an awareness, a self-reflective I-need-to-step-back moment, an illusion of control. But then there is being pulled toward the edge again, and the never-ending role reversal of master and slave that comes to represent addictions.

TIER THREE

Tier 3 is the other majority. It's the TEs that people draft or pick up because they need a TE when their TE1 is on bye week. They are TE2s, and occasionally they erupt for a big game and TE1 status. These are your Eric Ebrons or Hunter Henrys. There are a lot of these types of players, and along with kickers and defense/special teams, they usually make up the last few dreaded can-we-log-off-already rounds of a fantasy football draft.

In my fantasy sports addiction tiering system, this is still a healthy percentage and may even be THE majority. It's unknown. But let's just call it an even 50 percent of the sixty mill who have fun, enjoy the social and camaraderie aspect, and don't feel even the slightest tinge or pull of addiction. These people don't need to watch every snap of every game, and they have no problem tuning out a Monday night game even when their own fantasy fate hangs in the balance. These people may spend a little time preparing for the draft, or they may spend no time at all. Probably, a lot of these players are women, though certainly Tier 1 and Tier 2 also have female representation.

A Tier 3 addict wouldn't dream of watching more than three hours of football on a Sunday. Checking their phone for an update is not in the forefront of their thoughts on a busy Sunday with Things To Do. They don't remember things like the time the Dolphins and Ronnie Brown used the wildcat formation and dominated the Jets on Monday Night Football, causing the Multiple Scorgasms to lose the matchup despite being ahead by 2 points going into the game versus the Stiff Arms with no players left, because the Jets D gave up so many points and yards that they actually scored negative 3 points. Tier 3 players play, mostly because their friends or significant others play. They have fun. And that's it. It's harmless.

TIER FOUR

The fourth tier for TE's is basically irrelevant. It exists. It's out there. But nobody ever talks about it, or writes about it, or thinks too much about it. I encourage a fantasy writer to try this experiment: Write an article entitled, "Combing the Depths: Penetrating the Subtle Nuances of the 4th TE Tier," and stand back and watch as exactly No One reads it ever.

Maybe two experts could even have a friendly wager over who could write a legitimate 4th tier TE article that would go the longest with zero clicks. It could last years and be very fulfilling.

Tier 4 in my Fantasy Sports Addiction Tier is basically the same: irrelevant, superfluous, in existence but not worth describing or writing about.

One site claims there are 2.5 million fantasy football leagues out there, which lines up with other estimates that there are something like 30 million fantasy football owners. If we look at just my league as a predictor, there is at least one hardline, multiple-league, daily-fantasy enthusiast, a Tier One-er, the Omega Moos (at least he acted like one, until he auto-drafted). Then there are a handful of debatable Tier 2 owners, including Show Me Your TD's, Honkey Lips, the Whiskey Ditkas, FAB Cheapskate, and 50 Shades of Jay. Lastly, there are your Tier 3 guys, the Thack Attack, Sayulita Express, the Deep Snake,

Six Years of College, Miami Schmolson, The Nils U, etc., who
play and are competitive and have a good time. We even had
a representative of the fourth tier (until he retired after ten
years) the Bluebirds, who occasionally left a roster spot open, like
when a kicker is pulled on a Sunday morning and then was openly
berated on the league message board by the Omega Moos.

This would seem to support my hypothesis that there are
about 2.5 million, on average one per league, Gronk-like,
freakishly addicted to fantasy sports deep-end, hooked
gamblers. Then you've got the second tier, on average two or
three per league—but which *might be* five or six— creating a
range of either 5 million on the low end or something like 12
million borderline addicts experiencing nuanced, subtle, and
even surreptitious psychological effects from a supposedly
harmless distraction.

A CASE STUDY

Profiles exist of the Tier 1 Gronk-level addict. The guy who lost
his shirt on Fan Duel. Below this, however, exists a vacuum
of potentially millions. Here is someone who might fit that
description:

C.D. Carter is a blogger for the *New York Times* N.F.L. Blog,
and I think it would be safe for a psychologist using my tier
system to put him in Tier 2 with an occasional foray into Tier 1.

Here's how he starts a 2012 blog about his addiction: "I
cannot watch football the way it was meant to be watched. I
watch for stats. I fret about fantasy points, not game outcomes.
The game, in short, is meaningless."

He goes on to say he doesn't watch the playoffs and doesn't
care about the Super Bowl. He has loyalty to no one but himself
and his pretend roster of random players. His obsession crowds

out his ability to feel joy or pain from a real team. Even from his fantasy team, he feels no joy—there's only anxiety, pain, and disappointment. When he wins, he's happy not to lose. When he loses, he's crushed.

He's immersed in Twitter. He has a side gig writing about fantasy. Devouring fantasy stats for hours floats his boat. So in the words of Sheryl Crow, "If it makes you happy, it can't be that bAAAAAaaaaaaAAAaaad." Yet he knows he's on the verge of it being that bAAAAAaaaaaaAAAaaad.

In fact, presumably for the blog posting and *just* the blog posting, he spoke with Kim Young, a licensed psychologist, psychology professor at St. Bonaventure University, and founder of the Center of Internet Addiction. She concurs that internet addictions like fantasy sports are hardly different from other web-based vices (a long hallway here of things that I'm just going to breeze right by), but that online addictions "stem from a desperate need to control an outcome— any outcome." The driving force, she says, is an illusion of control.

Dr. Young basically rubber stamps the whole brain-dopamine-reward-system similarity between fantasy sports and other more serious, SERIOUS addictions like crack and heroine, including this little nugget: "Changing neurotransmitters creates altered psychological states that bring euphoria to an addict's ravaged brain," which Carter relates to when he is "scouring the waiver wire." (This is likely the first time the words "waiver wire" and "ravaged brain" ever appear together in the same paragraph.)

Carter shares some stories of other addicts and goes on to quote Chris Wesseling, senior N.F.L. editor at Rotoworld, one of the behemoths of the fantasy sports industry. Wesseling says there's not much separating fantasy football and Dungeons and Dragons, and that fantasy football is a game for nerds. He says there should be shame (which is odd for one talking about his own profession) and that "nobody cares about your fantasy team except you." This last one is verifiable by anyone who has ever tried to relate a fantasy football yarn to someone not in the league, like a spouse. Look closely and you can actually watch the listener's eyes glaze into lifelessness.

Carter closes his blog with the revelation that his wife is due to have a baby and he hopes becoming a parent will give him the perspective to return fantasy football to its rightly place near the bottom of Life's Priorities. He just wants a normal relationship with fantasy football, he claims.

SO NOW WHAT?

The first stage is awareness. Many Tier 2 addicts probably have some level of awareness that fantasy sports has a little too much control of their day-to-day life, exerts too much power on their mood, and is just simply too much of a time suck. Possibly, the Tier 2 addict is like blogger C.D. Carter and just wants, "a normal relationship with fantasy sports."

If you were to take your concern to a licensed psychologist, as Carter did under the guise of journalism, what would the therapist say? Kimberly Youn vuit. Which brings us back to where we started, with Bono's paradox.

A fantasy sports Tier 2 addict can't live with or without fantasy sports. Up and quitting is like the drug addict who now has the dopamine reward/pleasure circuits sitting like ghostly roller coaster rails at an abandoned amusement park in the brain, falling into disrepair from neglect. There's no more highs or lows—just empty, unused rails in the brain. Ravaged. The cold turkey former owner of the Kuppets or Yippee Ki-Yay Justin Tucker now has to build new ones, because life is a little more boring. Especially come early September when all your friends are heading to the draft room, or maybe even a destination trip/guy's weekend, as is custom in some leagues.

Maybe, like the creator of fantasy sports, former *NY Times* editor Daniel Okrent that simply walked away (for good the second time), the Tier 2 addict won't miss it. Maybe they come around to appreciate, as Okrent did, the "sheer joy and beauty of the game." Sort of a less-is-more, everything-is-nothing kind of eastern spiritual peace.

Or maybe there is a normal relationship, a New (Fron)Tier (see what I did there?) out there for fantasy sports players, in between Delaney Walker and Cody Fleener: some way to keep fantasy sports near the bottom of Life's Priorities, where it can't usurp time, money, energy, MOOD, and self, but still be fun *and* competitive.

What would this (Fron)Tier look like? First, it would knock fantasy fandom down below sports fandom. This means rooting for the Cubs over the Orphans (or whatever your fantasy baseball team is named), which really is more compelling, rewarding, interesting, and social. When the Cubs won the World Series, I talked about this with practically everyone everywhere. When the Orphans didn't win, I talked about this with exactly one person, the owner of Landau Calrissian. This is rooting for the Bears over whatever I name my team this year (leaning towards the Oompa Loompas, a reference to a Bears halfback passing play named after Tarik Cohen). This is following the NFL season. This is loving the pure story and drama and fun of it: thirty-two separate sagas unfolding in a Shakespearean dance of comedy, tragedy, and, sometimes, real triumph that cities and communities and families take pride in, come together around, experience joy because of, and remember for a long, long time—like the '85 Bears. This is much more interesting on a human level than any fantasy legend. It's like comparing real-life tragedy (on or off the field) with how Darletta's Lasagna Burps missed the playoffs through a tie-breaker, which is really no comparison at all.

The second part will be deeply personal for each player, but it involves discipline and overcoming the master/slave dynamic. Basically, it's creating some Rules To Live By, not unlike an AA program. Similar in that it must involve some clichés, but different in that there isn't really a PROBLEM, not yet anyway, just something festering that needs to be put in its place.

For example, the New (Fron)Tier addict might place a limit on how many times he can glance at his phone for updates on his team. Like when he's checked it at 12:34 p.m., there's no need to check it again at 12:38 to see if Ellsbury scored from third base or if Greinke got out of that two-on-two-out jam. Maybe even putting time limits on waiver searches, etc. Making sure that everything else more important—basically *everything* else—is done and complete before indulging. It's this humble fantasy sports player and writer's opinion that DFS should just be avoided altogether, much like I would advise someone who smokes pot habitually and responsibly to avoid cocaine.

Third—and this isn't as concrete or specific— it's kicking to the curb with a heel to the face the pathetic dweeb loser; the PPR and non-PPR insecure, the low self-esteem, needy dork geek, inflated egotistical schmuck that hangs any kind of figurative or psychological hat on anything that has anything to do with fantasy sports at all. Because it's all basically luck and a crapshoot, and anyone who says different, well-healed or otherwise, is full of it.

This way, the New (Fron)Tier fantasy sports aficionado can return fantasy sports to its rightful place at the bottom of Life's Priorities, keep it there, and enjoy it, while still appreciating things like the athleticism of an Omega Moo-owned Odel Becham Jr. catch or the speed of a Chapman fastball when he's pitching against the Orphans. And then along with moments come the *stories*: the captivating reality TV that is the epic journey of each team of gladiator-like athletes through the odyssey of a professional sports season. With these basic steps, losing isn't so crushing, but allows for a sense of humor to take over so you can laugh. With someone. It's social. It's the best of both worlds. It's fun and healthy without the *Really?*

It's with *and* without you. And the and is you give yourself away.

SOS IN THE JURY LOUNGE

What follows is a collection of thoughts and observations that landed on me, my imagination and sense of humor and curiosity drifting like an over-sized bird just a little too weak to make any real progress in the strong vector of Now. It hovered over me all day, leaving little droppings and figurative doodies, all while I waited at the Vista Superior Court to be selected for jury duty.

These splats have been recorded, reproduced, and discarded here like a Potential Juror's message in a bottle, to float and drift where Chance and Time and Prevailing Currents may take it, to hopefully one day arrive on the distant shore of a Jury Lounge, to at long last arrive in the hands of another Potential Juror.

I sat way off to the back, in the corner and side of the large, well-lit room that is the Jury Lounge, in a section with tables and chairs as opposed to the long rows of theater-like seating. Monday through Thursday these rows are slowly and politely filled with somnolent, evenly spaced-out Potential Jurors randomly drawn from all walks of life.

My point of view basically bisected the Quiet Area, a separate room with windowpane walls, also with tables and chairs. The Potential Jurors' reflections appeared in the Quiet Area panes that I looked through, the apparitions transparent and ghost-like, also mingling with reflections of the Outside World and entrance behind me, more phantasmal people with court business to attend to coming in and out of my double-paned portal view of the front podium, where both the judge and the juror administrative assistant made opening remarks and speeches.

THREE *WHAT IFS*

1) What if, instead of polite nods and humorless chuckles and silence vulnerable to crickets, instead of this response from myself (as well as all the other Potential Jurors), what if instead of the silent non-response to their banal jokes—jokes that they presumably make every day, day in and day out, small jokes like, "To pick up your hefty jury duty check…" and "In the back right are time cards and a time clock if you need proof for your employer that you did in fact have jury duty; these also can be used for spouses" and others that were so banal that they've escaped my memory. What if, instead of the Silent Treatment and humorless smiles— the kind of smile you give for a photo you'd as soon not be in— what if these little administrative pokes at humor were instead greeted by a Potential Juror way back in the corner behind the two separated-paned walls of the Quiet Area with loud and intense heckling, serious hissing and booing that would make even the most seasoned stand-up comic tremble? Something along the lines of "YOU SUCK! BOOOO! TERRIBLE!!"

2) After the opening remarks, I was standing in the hallway outside the J Lounge and snacking on an apple in the bright morning sunlight streaming through the windows to the

Outside World. I observed a middle-aged female Potential Juror stroll out and ask a twenty-something woman working the snack bar, "Can I use my phone?"

The twenty-something woman, with the full might and authority vested in a Jury Lounge snack bar attendant, yet without so much as a glance at the five other Potential Jurors all standing around, glued to their phones, said, "Sure."

What if instead, this twenty-something bored J Lounge snack bar attendant responded with, "ARE YOU CRAZY? PUT THAT SHIT AWAY!"

3) What if, after a bathroom break, one in which I brought my computer, backpack, and headphones (but left behind a notebook and coffee mug to preserve my spot) to the pristinely clean J Lounge men's room, what if I also left behind and deliberately put my headphones out on the table, my very large Sony noise-canceling MDR-NC7's, in PLAIN SIGHT, impossible to miss, large leather ear pads and tangled cord dangling. And upon returning, what if I cried hysterically, "MY HEADPHONES! WHERE ARE MY HEADPHONES? HAS ANYONE SEEN MY HEADPHONES? SOMEONE TOOK MY HEADPHONES!" And just went on, hysterical and berserk, until someone asked the inevitable question: "Are those your headphones, sitting right there?"

TWO HAPPENINGS FROM THE J LOUNGE: ONE COINCIDENTAL AND ONE SAD

Coincidental. At a circular table not eight feet away from me in the back and side corner section with tables, lo and behold, all of a sudden comes and sits my old Pal, principal César M. The very Pal who "had to let me go" at the end of the 2010-2011 school year with full knowledge of my pregnant wife and new house situation.

I sat in his line of sight, presuming he would turn his head fifteen degrees to the left, which he did not, to my knowledge, do, for the first thirty minutes, so in effect I sat just fifteen degrees out of his precisely linear, straight-ahead line of sight, eight feet away, for the first forty-five minutes of the Jury Selection process, which included two speeches, a video, and roughly twenty minutes of kill time.

This forty-five-minute stretch went by without so much as a nod of recognition or any body language that might pass as a form of greeting. Though, again, I can't claim that my old Pal ignored me, because I did not see him look even five degrees to the side—only either straight ahead or down. He's a very linear Pal, too, as I remember, so this seems plausible.

After the video, and the second direction from the juror administrative assistant, I went over and said, "Hey, César!" in a fancy-seeing-you-here kind of way.

To which he replied with the classic can't-quite-remember-your-name-though-I-know-I-know-you greeting, the very one I give to old students on occasion: "Heeeeeeeeyyyyy you!"

He fidgeted uncomfortably for the duration of our five-minute conversation, including at the 3:40 mark a squirming line about paperwork, which I followed up with a question about his new Pal position and the new school, which led to 1:20 more about how it will be the first year with seniors at the new school.

Transition from Coincidental to Sad: Thirty minutes later, with another ninety minutes of kill time before either one of us would be called, my old Pal finished up his paperwork and began reading.

Sad. Five minutes into old Pal César M.'s reading, suddenly, lo and behold, sits down next to him at the table directly in front of me and my line of sight, a young man with a strabismic, Born Last Night kind of expression. Observing him as he chatted with my old Pal, it appeared that BLN was not skilled in reading social cues and may be on the spectrum for a social-reading-cue type of disorder. It took my old Pal close to five full, clearly excruciating minutes before he was successfully able to retreat back to his book with any kind of reading-full-sentences type of success. The next five minutes, though, I doubt he was able to make it through a paragraph of his presumably work/education/being-productive-and-career-oriented-on-a-weekday related text, as BLN continued to interject God only knows what (I observed the conversation with eyes only, as I had my very large Sony noise-canceling MDR-NC7's jamming away some jazz tuneage). Finally old Pal was able to turn a page, and BLN moved on to old Pal's neighbor who, with much more social dexterity than my old Pal, was able to retreat into *Killing Reagan* in a matter of a minute.

So BLN got up and was on the move. It wasn't long before he settled into the row directly in my line of sight, behind my old Pal, and latched onto a retired woman. During this entire process, I continued to observe by sight only, so again could only begin to imagine what BLN and this retired lady discussed during their roughly forty-five-minute conversation (I did happen to catch that she was retired, between tunes; one reason that I can speculate that BLN falls on a communication spectrum was his loud tone and lack of any control or awareness whatsoever as far as volume goes).

The administrative assistant came up to call the first group of Potential Jurors selected. César was in this pool. He gave me a very professional, good-luck-in-your-day-of-jury-service-as-well as-educational-career, nod/toothless smile. Fifteen minutes later, with BLN and the retired woman still sputtering along, the admin assistant called the second group, of which both BLN and myself were selected. I observed the slightly awkward, goodbye-now exchanged between them.

My group of some forty-plus selected jurors walked slowly to the elevators, not unlike a group of tourists in Disney's *Haunted Mansion*. As some filed in, we waited for the next elevator and the next proximal group to file in. That's when I noticed that BLN had latched on to a nearly identical, though different, presumably retired lady.

The whole thing struck me as sad because it occurred to me that the two different retired ladies BLN spoke with seemed lonely—not just mildly bored and up for some friendly chitchat with a stranger, but like desperate-to-talk-to-another-being-with-a-pulse lonely.

IN THE COURTROOM

A clerk gave us all numbers and assigned seats in the courtroom. The first twelve sat in the Juror's Box. The next twenty-four sat in the Box Next To The Juror's Box. And the final twelve sat in the Box Next To The Box Next To The Juror's Box. I was #40 and in the front row of the Box Next To The Box Next To The Juror's Box.

There was a mix-up involving BLN when a Young Guy with a similar-sounding name followed the group from the J Lounge and up the elevators. When his name wasn't called by the clerk, this Young Guy sought to clarify the situation. The clerk came into the courtroom with Young Guy and called out number six and BLN's name, to sort it all out. Turns out BLN #6 was in the right and Young Guy, despite having a very similar-sounding name was alas, not on the list. The clerk told the Young Guy to head back down to the J Lounge and wait for his name to be called (again). Young Guy responded with a very Young Guy-sounding, "Oh, OK. It's cool. No problem." Like it was up to him to determine the existence of a problem. BLN, on the other hand, responded to the clerk calling out his name with something approaching abject terror—like he might be found guilty of a crime on the spot.

• • •

It was my first time being in a real court of law. It's just like on TV, with the bailiff and the flags and the court reporter typing away furiously. The lighting was very good, bordering on obnoxiously bright. The place was immaculately clean and orderly. On the wall was a painting of Lady Justice, blindfolded and holding-a-balance. The suited attorneys sat at two nice broad wooden tables facing the regal and stately bench. The defendant, an older Hispanic man, sat meekly beside his attorneys with his back to us and never once moved. Not even a muscle. Then there was the whole, "please rise for the Honorable Judge So-And-So" bit. The bailiff was very fit and carried a gun. The judge entered in a black robe and instructed us all to be seated.

I listened as the judge wasted absolutely no time and got right down to business giving very official, professional, legal-proceeding and explanatory business-like remarks. The case involved some sort of elderly abuse. Following the judge's opening instructions were brief introductions from the public prosecutor (a young woman, tall, thin, with long, wavy brown hair) and one of the two defense attorneys (both young men, one tall and bearded, the other short and clean-shaven, or just facial-hairless in a young man kind of way). The short one gave the opening remarks. He seemed to be some sort of a protégé. His first remarks were on the diffident side. The judge asked him to speak up. He paused once during his remarks to consult the taller attorney, who was seated. This would become a pattern: He did most of the talking but would frequently be on the listening end of a whispered conversation.

Then it was the Potential Jury's turn. Juror #1 was given a microphone. There were laminated questionnaires under their seats. They were instructed to answer the routine, general questions on a matter-of-fact, pertinent, the-court-needs-to-know basis. All the Potential Jurors in the Box and the Box Next To The Box had to answer them. Those of us in the Box Next To The Box Next To The Box were not provided with the laminated forms.

The questions were like, "How old are you? What kind of work do you do? Have you, or anyone in your family, ever been accused or convicted of a crime? Have you ever served on a jury before? Do you have any friends in the criminal justice system? Do you have any personal experience with elder abuse or physical abuse of any kind that would prevent you from being impartial in this case?"

The judge then reiterated that there was, "No need to go into personal details that you are uncomfortable sharing."

I learned more about BLN #6 when it came to be his turn to speak into a mic and answer. I learned by the shaking of the laminated questionnaire that BLN is EXTREMELY nervous speaking in front of people. We all learned (we being the 48 Potential Jurors, the judge, the district attorney, the clerk, the bailiff, the two defense attorneys, and the defendant) that BLN has little experience speaking into a microphone and found it even more difficult to control the volume of his voice, that he is unemployed, that he has no friends in the legal or law enforcement professions, that he feels he could be impartial, and something about a DUI that the judge was able to clear up: His father got a DUI six years ago.

About ten of the Potential Jurors in the box answered the questions, then the judge called an hour for lunch recess, reminding us not to discuss the case with anyone outside the courtroom.

TWO MORE WHAT IFS

1) What if I really tested, and I mean really, the judge's stern admonition not to talk to the attorneys during the lunch recess if you happen to cross their path. The temptation presented itself when one of the defense attorneys, the shorter clean-shaven one, walked into the very Rubio's where I sat eating a California bowl, a "salad" with essentially no lettuce.

What if I went over to get some more mild red salsa and approached him in the growing line with "Hey! Isn't this something? You and I. Together. The same courtroom and the same case. And the same Rubio's. How's that for a coincidence? Tim Miller, Juror #40.

"You should order a California bowl—not that it's a salad even if it's on the 'Salads' part of the menu. I know the judge said don't talk and all, but he has to say that, right? Right. I mean, shit. Here we are. Wow. Can you give me some of the deets? What's up with this case? Do you think he's guilty?"

And then, post-order, maybe make it a little personal as he ignores me while waiting for his food to just be ready already. "What was with that intro you gave in the courtroom, anyway? Is this your first case? You seemed a tad nervous, not exactly wet-your-pants nervous, but still definitely on the nervous side."

Then I might follow him to his car. I can imagine him walking quickly, burrito in hand, just trying to get the fuck away from me.

"Playing it cool. Good call. You never know when or where that prosecutor might be watching. I feel that there's some sexual tension between the two of you. Just me? OK— see you in a few! Good talk. Are you on Facebook?"

2) Also, what if I tested this with the young and tall prosecutor when she knocked on the courtroom door after lunch and had to (slightly impatiently) wait for the bailiff to open the door for three or four somewhat awkward minutes as she was surrounded by Potential Jurors. What if I sauntered over and leaned in with, "Knock knock. Who's there? Juror. Juror (pronounced "d'yer") bailiff change the locks again? No, only kidding. Hi. Tim is my name, #40. Interesting case we have here. It's my first time in a real courtroom. So clean and well-lit. I don't know why but it feels like I'm back in high school. All these quote-unquote rules you're supposed to follow. Don't run in the hallways. Don't be late to class. Don't smoke weed in the bathroom. Don't talk about the case while on lunch break. More like, don't get caught, right? But what's he gonna do if say like, you got locked out and some juror that's not even in the box *next to* the box next to the juror's box walks up and asks for a little 4-1-1, just to be in the know. I mean they don't even give a guy a laminated form to prepare his responses and suddenly he can't make small talk while the bailiff is doing who-knows-what and you're out here stuck. I mean sheesh. (Then, what if the door opened and the prosecutor entered without a word?) Good talk. Not about the case, but you know, stuff. What did you have for lunch by the way? I'm guessing probably not lasagna. That's the last thing you want to eat before getting back to work.

MORE DUTY

The sign, a sheet of white paper taped to the wall, outside the security screening line, said in bold, typed letters, "NO LIQUIDS IN THE MACHINE. PLEASE HANDLE." However, as people walked in the north entrance, there was a security TV screen facing the security guards and obscuring the "NO," so in effect it said, "LIQUIDS IN THE MACHINE. PLEASE HANDLE."

After again observing the security guards instruct three or four Potential Jurors in front of me in line to hold onto their water or coffee (first in the morning and then for a second time as I returned from lunch), I thought about informing them of this fact, this perspective they might not have from their side. But after watching them in action for another moment I thought better of it, as they seemed exactly like the last people on earth who need to be told how to do a job.

AN INCIDENT THAT MAY COME TO BE A MICROCOSM OF THIS ENTIRE ESSAY/ MY LAST THREE YEARS OF WRITING

When I got back into the elevator after lunch, I held the door for a white-haired guy who walked, carried himself, shaved, combed his hair, tucked his ironed shirt in, and wore Jury Badge #19 in a way that clearly communicated he didn't take one iota of B.S. from anyone ever. I hit the button for the second floor on accident, when the courtroom was in fact on the third floor.

When the door opened on two, I quickly hit the "close door" button and started to mutter/babble something incoherent to NO B.S. #19 about forgetting the floor and my mind being elsewhere with all the dead time, but I stopped mid-mutter because a woman got on our elevator from the second floor, and I almost closed the door on her. Then she reached over and pushed the button for the first floor, so that we began descending. Once the woman got out and two more people settled in, I pressed the button for the third floor and the elevator began ascending again. NO B.S. #19 shot me a glance like I shouldn't take drugs and my formless puddle of a person consisted entirely of liquid waste, disgraceful to my parents, community, and nation.

Getting off the elevator, I had the sad and somewhat serious thought that this entire notebook of splats, along with everything I've written the past few years—published and unpublished—was in some way equivalent to my cut-off mutter/babble, and that most people out there in the random Jury Pool world were somehow more like NO B.S. #19 than the sympathetic, open, and attentive friend I imagined I was writing to. And that, instead of reading and appreciating and maybe even learning or laughing, that most readers would have the STOP FUCKING WITH MY ELEVATOR BUTTONS reaction of #19.

• • •

While waiting in the hall after lunch as the DA avoided eye contact and knocked for the second time on the door, BLN stared around and looked at people with an almost puppy-like supplication to talk/be friends. He had his hair parted to one side so that it flopped over his face. He had to keep flipping his head to keep it out of his strabismic eyes, which were behind black thick-rimmed glasses that only lacked a piece of white tape in the middle. He wore his #6 badge and carried a bike helmet, backpack, and water bottle.

It was easy to imagine that BLN had limited experience in both legal and just general being-around-people settings. The contents of his very full backpack, on the other hand, were difficult to imagine indeed.

He soon latched again, this time to #28, a late-twenties Hispanic guy. #28 was absorbed by his phone, but BLN managed to engage him about the very thing on the phone that had #28's attention. #28 didn't seem to mind that much, but also his primary attention and focus throughout the exchange remained his phone, and BLN firmly remained secondary. #28's gestures and small comments directed at BLN resembled a person watching television and periodically patting his dog.

After using the restroom, I walked past BLN, who commented on my Beatles T-shirt.

"That was a great band!" he said without any trace of understated irony.

• • •

Back in the courtroom after lunch, the mic continued to circulate as the Potential Jurors in The Box and the Potential Jurors Next To The Box answered the routine, generic and gently probing questions. The judge took a moment to assure me and the rest of the Potential Jurors in the Box Next To The Box Next To The Juror's Box that we were important, too. That we mattered and our service was just as valid. The judge's tone and speech were always very practical and businesslike. I wondered if he had a hard time changing gears at home, or if maybe he sometimes unconsciously slipped into this voice at dinner.

"And now we're going to move from the Salad Portion of the meal to the Main Course. Before we do that, does anyone need any more silverware? This is also an opportunity to refill beverages. Once we move forward, there will be no moving back to the salad eating portion of the meal. At no time will you be allowed to use salad dressing on the main course, including ranch. Very well. And thus the Salad Portion is concluded."

At one point things got pretty uncomfortable and awkward for just about everyone involved, though the judge and attorneys and other people who do this every day were clearly used to these sorts of exchanges. Basically #12, a retired nuclear physicist, volunteered waaaaaaaayyyyy tooooooo muuuuuuuch personal information on the final question. There's no need for any details or depth here other than to say he wrapped it up with, "When someone beats the crap out of you for fifteen years, sure it has an effect on you."

We took a fifteen-minute break for the judge to talk to the attorneys, and I decided to pace the hallway prisoner/philosopher-style and listen to tuneage. On my first pass, BLN sat off by himself, again with that puppy-like expression of supplication. By my third trip down and back, he was fully engaged in discussion with three older woman that, based on the body language and gesturing, may have had something to do with his bike helmet, public transportation, or routes to the courthouse.

I figured they would call us in soon, so I hung out in a patch of sunlight streaming in from the wall-length windows. I looked to the immediate Potential Jurors near me and sort of wished I could shake off both my post lunch fatigue and my introvertedness, put down the book and tuneage and start up some conversation of my own, but everyone was on some sort of device. I had some tired thoughts about all that lugubrious loneliness that I had been associating with Jury Lounges and DMV waiting rooms and other vast public government rooms and thought maybe BLN had something going: that it was better to be open and friendly and curious, even if naive, compared to busy and experienced and shut off from people. I watched BLN with new eyes, like he had something to teach me. The conversation he was having with his current crop of retired ladies was now almost certainly about the benefits of wearing a helmet while cycling.

Soon enough we were back in the courtroom, and the questions moved from the laminated questionnaire and a passing mic, to attorneys asking general questions and having people raise their hand or nod to agree or disagree. The prosecution went first. Sometimes an attorney would ask a follow-up, like, "Why do you feel that way, #8?" And #8 would respond in his normal voice while the mic was being passed and would arrive at his seat just as he concluded his remark. Mostly it was somewhat dull, with the most action being when the bailiff sprung to life to change the batteries on the mic that always arrived a moment too late. But one time it made it with plenty of time to spare and then didn't work, so the bailiff surged forward.

While changing the batteries he dropped one, and I imagined that for some of his days— probably fine by him— this was all the action that he saw.

"How was your day, dear?"

"Good. Changed the batteries on the mic again."

I started to relate to the mic, in terms of being needed, overall effectiveness, and contributing to the proceedings.

Things heated up when the shorter, clean-shaven defense attorney came forward. The attorney asked the jurors to imagine if their significant other was planning a trip to Las Vegas, solo, and "you asked this significant other if he or she would be faithful?"

He paused here, effectively. Then with the room leaning toward him, he added, "And your significant other said, 'Probably.' Would you be OK with that?"

Another pause. "No, you wouldn't. And it's in this same way that we don't want jurors here to think they could 'probably' be impartial."

After some whispers, the defense attorney offered some generalities about the case involving elder abuse, reminding the courtroom that he was prohibited from getting into specifics. Basically, he wanted to know if anyone would have an issue with self-defense as a defense for someone just shy of sixty-five. It was at this point that things got downright testy with #12, the retired nuclear physicist who had a history of abuse getting straight up combative with the defense attorney. "You're being very vague." "Can't you explain it better? I mean, you're an attorney." But the attorney again responded that he was prohibited from giving specifics about the case and tried to stick to a general, would-it-be-O.K.-to-fight-back inquiry, which #12 with his history wasn't buying or even budging on. So they went round and round in the old human circle of misunderstanding with all of us watching and listening and even the judge getting a little impatient.

As the DA and #12 danced around, it became clear that a lot of people in the jury box did not follow the expression "just shy of sixty-five years old," as in short of sixty-five. You could see perplexing looks, like they wanted to ask, "Why would you be shy of that?" To remedy this, the attorney made some allusion to the fact that he is from Ohio and in Ohio you get a buckeye when you turn sixty-five, not clearing things up at all and only adding to the judge's ire.

It all continued in this herky-jerky mostly communicating but not always to everyone, process. I tried to stay sharp and follow along and do my part to be prepared to get called into the Box Next To The Box. Finally, they got to the part where the attorneys thank the potential jurors in the box for their service but dismiss them as not conducive to their case or some other polite, euphemistic language.

Both sides took a turn dismissing. Then they called Potential Jurors from the Box Next To The Box and each side had to agree. BLN and, obviously, the nuclear physicist and some others were sent home.

The jury was set and everyone in the Box Next To The Box and the Box Next To The Box Next To The Box were thanked and dismissed also.

TWO FINAL SUMMATIVE BIG SPLATS

As I headed out into the hallway and onto the elevator with the other dismissed Potential Jurors, descending, it seemed like the time to be human and think Big Picture Thoughts, sort of culminating, reflective, what-does-today-mean-anyway thoughts. I glanced at their faces and thought they might be thinking something along the lines of my first Final Splat: that the world really is a stage and you never know when your number will be called for a Big Role, but that a lot of the time there are just too many people and not enough roles so many days are like today, where you are a spectator, an audience member, a Potential Something with a seat to observe the proceedings and make sense of it all. Basically, an extra.

It pays to pay attention though. You never know when you might be thrust into the spotlight. Or put on trial, for that matter.

The second Final Splat that occurred to me was like an end-of-a-long-day's-work satisfaction that I had served something larger than myself. Something important and fundamental and necessary. Something serious like the bedrock of our justice system. But inextricably linked to this is that the process of selecting the jury, the sitting around and waiting and listening and being randomly selected and walking into an elevator like *The Haunted Mansion* at Disneyland, followed by laminated questions and microphones and taking a lunch break and killing more time, the whole business—right up until you are actually on a jury and deciding someone's fate, or being sent home— is basically the adult version of a Saturday high school detention.

A BRIEF COMPARISON

I've done both on multiple occasions. Receiving the jury summons in the mail fills me with the exact same sense of apprehension and dread as when one of the Deerfield High School security guards, either Josephine (short, amorphous, looking unobtrusively through thick dark-rimmed glasses with protruding lower jaw and gap between front teeth, kind but in a don't-mess-with-me venomous manner, in her standard uniform of navy blue pants, blue vest, white short-sleeved button-down shirt, silver pin-on high school security guard badge, and one of those weird ties that's like a band of cloth that snaps together— this along with a tall coif of orange hair) or Bob (tall, middle-aged, balding, in blue pants, white shirt, black tie that never quite reached the belt due to his slight middle-aged paunch, and matching silver badge), stopped by my first period World Civilization classroom and served me with a small blue slip, a notice of time and date and length of sentence, either two, four, or the dreaded six hours of Saturday detention.

When you arrive, there's the same mild curiosity about the other human specimens who have been selected to attend.

Though in Saturday school, there's the obvious difference of each student having committed some sort of an offense, a what-are-you-in-for reason for being there (like the ones I perpetrated to receive Saturday school: throwing an apple across the cafeteria, being habitually late to Spanish, not serving a previous detention, or ditching study hall).

In jury duty there is just the random nature of being selected (sort of like you've been caught in a net that swooped up) and finding a day and time that fits within your schedule.

The sweet spot in the comparison is the overwhelming need to kill time. Reading, (home)work, puzzles, crafts—anything to keep the mind occupied. As a writer, it's reassuring to know that as long as there are free societies based on juries selected by peers, there will always be Jury Lounges and Potential Jurors who need something to read.

So they're basically the same day, except in the Jury Lounge, you're allowed to wear headphones, and you never know when they are going to call your name.

Looking back, a silver lining to those early experiences in the high school Breakfast Club was the exposure I received to systems of justice. After serving a six-hour Saturday, I definitely thought twice about hucking fruit across the cafeteria. It sure did make us laugh, though, waiting for the lunch lady to turn her head, then letting those apples fly. The wedges were good for side-arm curves.

The elevator reached the lobby. The security guards were all sitting around, chewing the fat. The snack bar attendant was gone. I glanced toward the now desolate Jury Lounge and had the slightly depressing thought that it wouldn't be long until I was back next year. Just then, one of the dismissed Jurors turned and asked another dismissed Juror, "So, do we have to stay until five?"

"No. Now you can go home."
"Oh good!"

BORBORYGMI

borborygmus bawr-b*uh-rig*-m*uhs*/
noun, plural bor·bo·ryg·mi [bawr-b*uh*-**rig**-mahy]. *Physiology.*

1. a rumbling or gurgling sound caused by the movement of
   gas in the intestines.

sys·tem ˈsistəm/ noun

1. a set of connected things or parts forming a complex whole,
   in particular.
2. a set of things working together as parts of a mechanism
   or an interconnecting network. noun: system; plural noun:
   systems; "the state railroad system"
3. a set of principles or procedures according to which something is done; an organized scheme or method.

The good doctor Jimmy has always been fascinated with
systems. When we lived together in Chicago after college, we
had a lot of them. A recycling system. A system for paying rent
and bills. A system for shopping for groceries a.k.a. twaks. And
he had a lot of systems of his own: a system and regimen for
handling allergies. A system for picking NFL games against the

spread. Everything seemed to be a system of some sort to Jimmy, something he could study, manipulate, observe, control. When he happened upon my Dopp kit, he said, "Is this your medicine system? It's terrible! No wonder you can't breathe. We need to take care of this and get you on a new regimen."

When we moved out, he moved in with his future wife and I got my own place on Southport. He came over and right away analyzed all of my systems. "Not a very efficient recycling system. Is this your coffee set up? You might need an upgrade, bud."

Jimmy also finds intrigue (and employment) in larger systems like healthcare systems, the American criminal justice system, the U.S. Postal Service, public education, the solar system, and body systems. The apex of his preternatural systemic captivation is, far and away, the digestive system.

This system, which is essentially a long tube with one end for eating, talking, breathing, and kissing, and another for defecation, is the subject of a not insignificant percentage of all text communication between Jimmy and me. Also, it forms what might be considered the inspiration or climax of the evening that runs, like a long tube itself, through this narrative.

There are two other things that you, the reader, should know from me, Your humble Narrator, about Jimmy, before the grumbling begins *en serio*. The first is that Jimmy can't sneeze. When he sneezes it's like a car that won't turn over. He cites a broken nose suffered in childhood as the reason that he holds it in: It hurts to sneeze. His sneeze usually begins abruptly, followed by a series of violent convulsions and involves a mist or spray. I don't know if the part about the broken nose is true, but I do know that it's always noteworthy to observe *another* observer observing Jimmy sneeze for the first time. The new observer's eyes widen, at first in alarm, as if a neurological event like a seizure is taking place. Then their eyes narrow into a look of curiosity and even fascination. Their expression will say something like, "So this is how this person I just met sneezes. Interesting."

The other thing is that Jimmy has a Ph.D. in psychology. So Your Narrator hopes to convey to you, the reader, the difficulty in reconciling these two Jimmys. There's the Jimmy who has worked for multiple years in the government healthcare system known as the United States Veteran's Affairs psychology department, helping U.S. soldiers returning from Iraq and Afghanistan, as well as older veterans, cope with PTSD, substance abuse, and other mental afflictions (no laughing matter); the Jimmy who currently works at a neurology clinic as a psychologist and carries on intimate conversations regarding people's deep and innermost thoughts and strife, as well as conducting research on head trauma and concussions and memory— essentially, the Jimmy of achievement and seriousness and VA experience. This Jimmy must be reconciled with the Jimmy who comes off the ski slopes and announces to everyone in the car, "Coffee. Cream. Shoog. Stat." The Jimmy that absolutely cranked Randy Newman's "I Love L.A." on a summer morning, post-surf drive along Coast Highway 101. And the Jimmy that sends me text messages like this:

> *Thought I clogged a work toilet today;*
> *last minute tho :) it got sucked down*

THE LIPS OF THE NIGHT

What was the date of the evening in question?

Saturday, January 16th, 2016, the night of the NFL Divisional Playoff round featuring the Green Bay Packers vs. the Arizona Cardinals.

Who attended?

Dr. Jimmy, me, and two friends who also live in the North County of San Diego and were raised in a northern suburb of Chicago, forming something of a human bolus. For the purposes of this narrative, the two other friends will be known as SD Chicagoan A (SDCA) and SD Chicagoan B (SDCB), respectively. SDCA also attended the alma mater of both Dr. Jimmy and Your Narrator, Indiana University, where he coincidentally sang a capella with a former college roommate of both Jimmy and Your Narrator, one Mark Hollywood. SDCA has his own business booking musicians on cruise ships, does very well for himself, is a golfing partner of mine, and occasionally sings the national anthem at major sporting events, like, for example, an L.A. Lakers game. Dr. Jimmy doesn't play golf with his scant and precious free time, but surfs instead. SDCB, like Dr. Jimmy, is in the business of helping people and like SDCA, he is a singer. A graduate of Miami University in Ohio, he is just starting to make his way as a therapist. It is unclear to Your Narrator how he spends his free time, but it is neither golf nor surfing.

It should be noted that all four attendees are well-educated members of the middle to upper class and come from families of good standing. Other similarities include: all four participants are white, between thirty-five and forty years of age, and have young children. (SDCB has one daughter, Dr. Jimmy has two sons, and SDCA and I each have two daughters.) So the human bolus has a lot in common, generally speaking.

One significant contrast with Your Narrator is that the other three members subscribe to the Jewish faith; Your Narrator has a subscription to the religion of Christianity, raised Presbyterian, currently attending a Christian church that to my understanding is non-denominational Christian. The subject of religion came up frequently throughout the evening, though not with any personal depth but in a general observational and in-practice context, e.g. orthodoxy, meats consumed, relatives, temples attended, rabbis known, other professional members of temples acquainted with, family observational practices, and bar mitzvahs. For the majority of these conversations Your Narrator remained silent but listened with interest.

Where did the group watch the game?

Rosati's, a Chicago-themed restaurant in Encinitas, California.

Why was this location and game chosen?

For a variety of reasons. Primarily, the time of the game worked with all parties' schedules and therefore received clearance from the respective significant others. The featured match-up happened to be the one of most interest to all party members, greater than Patriots-Chiefs, Panthers-Seahawks, and Broncos-Steelers, primarily due to the Green Bay Packers' status as rivals to the favorite team of all four members, the Chicago Bears. The Chicago Bears did not make the playoffs during this particular season of professional football; however, the Arizona Cardinals were at one time the Chicago Cardinals, and being founded in 1898, are the oldest continuously run professional football team, having played in Chicago until moving to St. Louis in 1960. Therefore, with a certain historical perspective (i.e. desperation), the Cardinals can be considered a Chicago team playing a rival city in an NFL playoff game.

The four members of the party also needed a reason to escape domestic responsibilities, to find relief from daily pressures and stresses that can be boiled down to "the grind" and, despite the various professional career paths chosen by the members, all involve the day-to-day labor of childcare, diapers, providing for a family, and being a patriarch.

Finally, there is the added desire by all four members

to maintain a connection with our collective roots and background, hence our maintained loyalty to Chicago professional sports teams and the region of Chicago, specifically the northern suburbs. In addition to the chosen contest of Green Bay Packers vs. Chicago Cardinals, the establishment of Rosati's in Encinitas boasts of being "authentic Chicago," therefore the visit had the added incentive of being a verification of authenticity by four transplanted Chicagoans.

Were the game and evening memorable?

Yes. On two counts. First, the game itself featured a string of impressive plays and compelling events. Secondly, an equally startling and amazing revelation regarding SDCB's digestive tract occurred apropos of nothing.

I'm torking now

Jimmy is not Dr. Jimmy's real name. It's a nickname that hails from our college days at old Indiana University in Bloomington. One of Mark Hollywood's friends from Minnesota called him Jimmy, on accident, on an evening of drinking. This friend continued to call Dr. Jimmy, "Jimmy," presumably by mistake. When we caught wind of the misnomer, we had what can be considered something of a field day with the error, and, as happens periodically, the name stuck.

At this point an interesting tangential digression can be made regarding this period and the general use of nicknames amongst Dr. Jimmy and Your Narrator's group of friends. One friend had a Serious Girlfriend, not particularly popular with the circle, who called members of the circle nicknames that were not in fact actual employed nicknames. For example, she used "Greaser" for a member of the circle with the last name Gries and "Benners" for a member with the first name

"Ben." On one hand, it provided a mirthful and rich source of humor and derision vis-à-vis nicknames, yet on the other hand, it represented the superficial and somewhat sad attempt by Serious Girlfriend to make lasting connections with the circle of her Serious Boyfriend, which one would think ultimately contributed to the couple's demise.

Just farted loud as fuck outside of my office and then looked over and a coworker is like 10 ft away

It happens in the blink of an eye. One day you are twenty-something and still figuring it all out, trying on different ways to be and live. And then you're thirty going on forty, married with children, and—forget figuring out ways to live, you just need to figure out how to subdue your one-year-old long enough to floss her teeth.

Jimmy and I were roommates for the twenty-something part. In some ways, we are still are: roomies laughing at each other's farts or a good, savory bit of cackle-worthy local news. Like when it rains in San Diego and a reporter will be at the beach saying, "It's raining here, Bob. All the people left when it started. Look behind me, you can see the rain hitting the sand. Back to you." Except instead of down the hall, now he is down the road.

As ol' CBass jokes, Jimmy and I go back like car seats, starting with both of us losing parents relatively young, which in a way gives us a mystical sort of brother-in-arms unspoken understanding. Losing a parent does that, even though we lost parents ten years apart. It's like we both suffered the same wound in some long-ago battle. We both went to IU and both majored in journalism and both waited tables and had to figure out what the hell we were going to do with a journalism degree in the early 2000s. We both grew up with the '85 Bears and Michael Jordan and Wrigley Field. We both got married around the same time and gave best man speeches at one another's wedding (mine may have been a tad on the long side, at least the trivia part). And we both ended up in San Diego.

Took a huge shit at work, clogged the toilet, unclogged the toilet w a plunger, and then left my phone on top of the tampon trash can

Dr. Jimmy's father was also a doctor. He was an ophthalmologist, or eye doctor, for the other NFL Chicago franchise, the Chicago Bears. When Your Narrator first made the acquaintance of Dr. Jimmy, in the relatively halcyon days of high school in Riverview, Illinois, Jimmy was "the kid who worked for the Bears." And worked for the Bears he did: pulling up the net behind the field goal at Soldier's Field; tossing balls in with tight underhand spirals (not as tight as Dr. Jimmy would have you believe, though) from the sideline to the referee during the game; going to Platteville, Wisconsin to work training camp in late July and early August.

When Dr. Jimmy first started to drive, his license plate said "NFL OD," which Your Narrator incorrectly assumed was a typo for, "NFL 00." Your Narrator regretfully teased Dr. Jimmy about his license plate not knowing 1) that "OD" stood for ophthalmologist doctor and 2) his dad was dying of cancer.

Taking dump 2…total mud fest

DOWN THE ESOPHAGUS GOES THE HUMAN BOLUS

In what order did the group arrive at Rosati's?

SDCA and Your Narrator arrived simultaneously, halfway through the first quarter, and collectively selected a table over a booth in the near empty restaurant, one that allowed all four members to have a good vantage point from which to view a large flat-screen television. Soon after, SDCB arrived. Dr. Jimmy arrived last.

What were the opening subjects of conversation?

How Arizona scored in the first quarter (M. Floyd). A misunderstanding between Dr. Jimmy and SDCB about SDCB's San Marcos residence and the possibility of a carpool with Dr. Jimmy (residing in Del Mar, in the opposite direction of San Marcos). Jokes were made about overcoming this distance and inconvenience out of a sheer desire to carpool. Also discussed: an illness of SDCB's child and the difficulty in leaving a sick child at home. The contrast between the Packers in the current playoff matchup and the Packers that lost to the very same Chicago Arizona Cardinals 38—8 on December 27. Rosati's Chicago locations. The menu in general and appetizers in particular, specifically fried mushrooms, which led to a collective reminiscence about Chicagoland's Brown's Chicken, their superlative fried mushrooms, and childhood. When all of this inevitably stalled, a new subject was broached: the ethical implications of Dr. Jimmy's trade in the NEJ Memorial Fantasy Football League, in which Dr. Jimmy, fantasy owner of the Sayulita Xpress, traded to Sinead O'Con (nickname), fantasy owner of Show Me Your TDs, Peyton Manning (a week before he got hurt) and Brandin Cooks for Cam Newton and Antonio Brown, with the caveat that O'Con executed the trade with the sole purpose of blocking another NEJ Memorial team, the

Omega Moos, from winning the championship.

What was the verdict?

Split. SDCA and SDCB disagreed on the fairness of the trade, with SDCB advocating the position that trades are a means of "screwing over other people" while SDCA recognized the potential conflicts with the ideals of fairness and a level playing field.

Was there any other subject matter of interest in the opening discussion?

Yes: trivia, with Your Narrator playing host. The subject being the history of the Chicago Cardinals and Chicago Staleys (currently the Chicago Bears), with information stemming from the assistance of Your Narrator's smartphone.

What is an example of the types of trivia questions and who answered them correctly?

Q: What point total do the Chicago Cardinals have the distinction of being the only team in American professional football history to score?

A: Exactly 4 points in one game. On November 25, 1923, the Cardinals lost to the Racine Legion 10—4. Answered correctly by SDCB.

Q: Where did the Chicago Cardinals play?

A: Comiskey Park. Answered correctly by Dr. Jimmy, though the answer was not corroborated immediately, with the information not being readily found on the Wikipedia page being used by Your Narrator, drawing the ire and consternation of Dr. Jimmy, a person with a fervent conviction that trivia questions should not be asked by people who do not have the answer readily available.

What happened next?

Your Narrator started to tell a tale of trivia being used as a deciding factor for riding in the passenger seat of one Richard Sniadecki's pickup truck on a vacation to New York that included skiing in Vermont, a visit to New York City, and a stay at the Sniadecki home on Lake George. Most notable and pertinent was when Sniadecki began a high-stakes, three-hour-car-ride question with, "What civil war general…" to which Dr. Jimmy immediately blurted, "William Tecumseh Sherman," literally before the question was even out of Sniadecki's mouth, which was the correct answer and resulted in an extended, uncomfortable sitting position on a footstool with essentially no leg room for Your six-foot-four-inch Narrator, along with a celebration by Dr. Jimmy that might be flagged as excessive in today's NFL.

Did SDCA and SDCB appreciate the story?

Not fully. For one thing, the story contains a certain You Had To Be There quality, not uncommon for a Dr. Jimmy and Your Narrator cackler, but also the telling of the story was interrupted by the waitress requesting our dinner order.

What was ordered?

Fried mushroom appetizers. A house salad (by Dr. Jimmy)—providing the other members with mild derision fodder. For the entrées, each member of the human bolus ordered an Italian Beef sandwich known as "The Chief." Further, in the spirit of authenticity verification, the group ordered one small Chicago-style deep dish sausage pizza to share, which was previously agreed upon as something of a group strategy.

Fuming out my exam room right now
Just wretched things

THE GRUMBLING STOMACH

Where did you leave off?

The human bolus had just ordered their appetizers and entrées. SDCA and SDCB, having both attended Glenbrook North High School, began discussing a shared acquaintance, while Dr. Jimmy and Your Narrator continued to relive the debacles surrounding the footstool in Sniadecki's truck, notably 1) Sniadecki losing his car keys in two feet of powder snow and the three hours he spent searching for them, only to end up empty-handed and covered in sweat, coming up for air looking strikingly like Gollum from *The Lord of the* Rings in a jacket vest; 2) the injury that Dr. Jimmy, on his first real ski trip, sustained on the last run down, a steep black diamond, on which Sniadecki famously misled Dr. Jimmy with, "It's the only way to the car;" and 3) the code red number two Jimmy had to painfully hold for roughly forty-five minutes—after a night of drinking, a breakfast of coffee and pancakes—and before skiing, squatting on a footstool with fecal matter he could barely contain, which required Sniadecki to pull in to the skier drop-off lane so that Dr. Jimmy could dash inside and take care of business.

Was that all they reminisced about?

No. They further discussed the quantity of corned beef sandwiches that Dr. Jimmy consumed on the trip and whether that quantity could be considered prodigious. This led to a separate lane in their memory stroll, one also taking place in a diner and after a night of drinking, but in Chicago and not on that east coast trip. It was a well-traveled lane in their collective memories: the tone and manner by which Sniadecki diffidently asked/reminded an attractive, well-endowed waitress about an undelivered chocolate milk he previously had ordered, where what he actually said was, "It's totally O.K., but when you have a moment, do you think you could bring me my chocolate milk?" but considering the aforementioned tone and manner, he might as well have said, "You forgot my yum-yum. Goo-goo, gaa-gaa. Boobies."

What was the group imbibing?

Beer: All four drank different San Diego craft beers.

New work shitters are amazing

This tube of an evening happened in the past. But for a few paragraphs, as long as the grammar police coast is clear, I'd like to shift into the present, to sit with Jimmy again and shoot the bull.

We are drinking beers, watching the game, and I am explaining to Jimmy about my current work pooping (or, as Jimmy likes to call it, the antithesis of eating) situation. SDCA and SDCB are talking about a mutual friend.

"I have, essentially, a very small poo window," I say. "I arrive at school at around 7:35. I have to be at the crosswalk by 7:45. Therefore I usually wait to have coffee until after the crosswalk, around 8:05, while I check my email. Then I have from 8:15 to 8:25 as a poo window. Kids arrive at my classroom at 8:25. Regardless. A lot of days, my poo window closes and I'm still sitting there, shitting. So now I have to cut it off, run out to my class, and walk around carrying it all morning. It's terrible. My poo window is literally very constrictive."

Jimmy is enjoying hearing about my predicament. He smiles broadly and takes satisfaction in hearing about my poo window.

"When I take a dump, my patients just wait," he says.

"My kids will wait—because what else are they going to do,

but I always hustle it up and get out there so they only wait a minute or two. I cut it off and rush out of the bathroom, coming around the corner to see twenty-five fourth graders and their slightly peeved teacher. I mean I get it. Anyone who has ever had to kill time with twenty-five elementary students up against a wall knows that you can only hold their attention for so long, no matter how intriguing you make Simon Says. I come around the corner with that post-poo light sweat, ignore my tardiness, and jump right in. Never mind what was happening literally sixty seconds ago. 'Let's get class started! Today, Circuits in Parallel!'"

Jimmy laughs. I tell him about how I share a shitter with around twenty-five women at my school.

"Isn't there a men's room?"

"Yeah, but it's in the lounge and I have to walk all the way across campus. Every minute counts, so I just use the staff restroom near my room."

I tell Jimmy about how people are always knocking politely, and how I always have to say, "Just a minute," but how I really want to say something along our own lines like, "Taking a giant tork." Jimmy laughs. I tell him about how my digestive system is now hard-wired for my poo window of 8:05 to 8:25 because of my other daily responsibilities that mandate I use the restroom during this time frame, like the Zoo Crew and lunch clubs. I tell him about how sometimes I miss the poo window and then can't poo until the next day despite the discomfort and resulting passing gas. Jimmy listens and laughs. I tell him about how when I leave a skid mark on the bottom of the bowl, I put a piece of TP over it and that's like my calling card. I tell him about a period of time when a long-term sub always had to poo at the same time I did and we competed for the bathroom. Jimmy invents a new phrase: poo nemesis. He tells me about his work shitters. He likes systems. Then he asks me about the latest surfboard he has texted me that is for sale on Craigslist, I think about all those waves I could be riding, and we slip into the past again.

Jimmy is a surfer and wants me to become a surfer. I checked my phone and email, and he has sent me the link to eight different surfboards on Craigslist in a ten-month span. I have surfed, perhaps a dozen times in my life, and basically each time I get my ass kicked. My first attempt, I swallowed a gallon of salt water, got pummeled, lost my sense of equilibrium, and passed out on the beach. Which wouldn't have been so bad if it wasn't my first-time meeting my future wife's extended family.

I've taken to primarily treating my surfboard like a bodyboard, though one time I stood up and rode a wave with a helping push of an instructor in Hawaii. Here is the pattern: paddle out, get exhausted, ride a wave in and biff, paddle out again, feel totally exhausted, and sit on my board, "enjoying being out there," before riding in on my tum-tum.

My reluctance to surf is based on the following factors: 1) my general status as a novice with regards to swimming abilities and lack of buoyancy considering my slender and bony over-six-foot frame; 2) the average temperature of the Pacific Ocean hovering in the mid-sixties and below for a majority of the year and my own medical history which includes episodes of atrial fibrillation, one of the primary triggers being submerged in cold water; 3) general procrastination, reluctance, and hesitancy to make the relatively minor financial commitment of purchasing a long board (as recommended on numerous occasions by Dr. Jimmy), a surf board rack for transporting surf boards on a vehicle and 4) the time to travel from the ocean to my house, surf, return, and shower is at a minimum two hours; 5) the sheer force and energy of the ocean in general and rip tides specifically; 6) swallowing an inordinate amount of salt water due to relative inexperience and a tendency to mouth breath; 7) sharks.

Still, I know at bottom that Jimmy is right (even if I don't openly admit it). Twenty minutes from our homes are magical carpet rides that Jimmy only wants me to experience, too, if I can get over the hump. Which is a defining character trait of the good doctor: he cares about people and their mental health.

J: Saturday or Sunday games?
YN: My emergency shrimp quesadilla shit from yesterday set an early, high bar in my annual journal of gross shits. Sat or Sun works for me.
J: LOL

What did the waitress bring to the human bolus?
Fried mushrooms and a salad for Jimmy.
Did everyone eat?
Yes. Everyone tried the fried mushrooms. Jimmy ate his salad and shared a portion with Your Narrator.
What was the verdict?
The mushrooms were good but did not meet the standard set by Brown's of Chicagoland circa 1980s nostalgia. These mushrooms were not as crispy. SDCA and SDCB determined that it was cute that Jimmy shared a portion of his salad with Your Narrator.
What was the score of the game?
At halftime the score was 7—6. The Packers added two field goals.
What was the conversation during halftime?
Dr. Jimmy told the group how he has an interview to be an independent concussion specialist at NFL games next year. He

would be one of three specialists called upon to evaluate a player for trauma to the head. The position would not be paid but would come with room, airfare, hotel, and attendance (on the field) to NFL games on the West Coast (San Diego, Seattle, San Francisco, Denver, Arizona, and maybe as far as Kansas City).

We were also informed that Jimmy would not have to wear a suit, but would likely dress business casual. And that Jimmy would have to renounce his fantasy team, Sayulita Xpress, and sign a waiver that would prohibit him from any gambling in any form, including all fantasy football. Here jokes were made on all sides involving such scenarios as not letting Aaron Rodgers back into a game even if he hadn't suffered even the faintest whiff of head trauma, or making Jay Cutler play even if he couldn't see straight after being suplexed by Ndamukong Suh.

Dr. Jimmy endured these jokes good-naturedly. SDCA asked how he got this opportunity, and Dr. Jimmy related how a neurologist and brain surgeon that he works with is the smartest person he's ever met. He has always been enamored, sometimes infatuated, with knowledge and learning. "It is literally astounding how much this person knows," Jimmy said. "But he's also like a normal guy who goes hiking and you can talk to. Amazing, though. So intelligent it's mind-boggling. He's sooooooo smart." At which point Your Narrator pointed out that, in Dr. Jimmy's eyes, this neurologist carries the weight and esteem that a Kardashian holds for the average millennial. "If he had a *Keeping Up with Dr. So-and-So* show, would you watch it?" Dr. Jimmy affirmed that he would, but without showing (much) appreciation for the joke.

I was technically right about the ice cream salt thing

Anyhow

There is a quality to Dr. Jimmy that is for lack of a better term, Walter Sobchakian. For those unfamiliar, Walter Sobchak is a character from the movie, *The Big Lebowski*. Walter is the best friend of the main character and protagonist (the Dude). He is divorced, a converted Jew, a Vietnam veteran who somehow manages to relate everything back to the war, and very stubborn on matters of principle. Jimmy is neither divorced, a veteran, or a converted anything. He is however, like Walter, VERY STUBBORN and IMPETUOUS at times, on principle.

As a self-published author not wishing to run afoul of copyright laws, Your Narrator cannot reproduce these quotes verbatim, however any fan of *The Big Lebowski* should at this point, for comparison's sake, repeat their favorite Walter quotes here. The quotes should include the terms, "split hairs," "calmer," "face down," and "toe."

Examples of Dr. Jimmy's stubbornness/impetuousness:

1. He refuses to pay for admission at any Chicago street festival. "I'm not paying for that shit. This is a public street. I pay taxes. I'm walking down the street. I'm not going to pay money to walk down a street that my taxes pay for."
2. When surfing in the Pacific Ocean or riding bikes in the streets of Chicago, Jimmy is likely to take off on his own, leaving the people he is with behind, including on several occasions his wife, getting so far ahead that he is out of sight. Jimmy narrowly concedes that he exhibits this pattern of riding, yet focuses on other people not being able to keep up.
3. Regarding an Ice Cream Lab that I do at the end of the school year with sixth-grade students in which they put a mixture of milk and sugar in a bag and put this bag in another bag of ice, water, and salt, Jimmy and Your Narrator entered a scientific discussion of why salt is used in the

mixture of ice and water. Dr. Jimmy gave an insufficient answer because he did not discuss the different freezing point of water once the salt is introduced, and instead focused on the milk freezing faster but without providing an adequate causal relationship, at least as far as Your Narrator's memory is concerned. Jimmy disputes this and even sent the above text message about the "ice cream salt thing" waaaaaay after the fact.

4. Jimmy will pursue a line of argument that can be essentially considered a moot point and then end his argument with the following statement: "Just saying," e.g. "I know you've had some heart rhythm issues, but the water is sixty degrees. You live in sixty-degree air all the time. I'm just saying."

5. On a recent excursion to a SD groggery, Jimmy shared a story about his son calling his son's cousin "a dick." Jimmy's son is four years old. Jimmy's in-laws are concerned, but Jimmy is not bothered by his son's language. "Look. The cousin was being a dick. What are you gonna do?"

6. After a round of golf to which Jimmy first declined the invitation, and later accepted, without communicating this properly to all pertinent members— giving rise to the phrase Another Jimmy Debacle (AJD)— he led the group to a dinner of burgers at a Local Burger Establishment. This meal consumed at the LBE preceded a Holiday Potluck Party (HPP) at Dr. Jimmy's *own* house, with a wide variety of vastly superior dishes to the burgers consumed at the LBE. Therefore, while the pertinent members of the golfing party stood around with little to no appetite, improperly dressed in golf attire for the formal HPP while Jimmy went upstairs to change, the phrase AJD went from newborn term to permanent and cemented and useful expression.

7. Your Narrator is unclear whether he has succeeded in

portraying the range and complexity of his friend: the generosity and intelligence and compassion to go with the tenacious stubbornness or, for lack of a better term, idiocy. (This is used with affection—sometimes Jimmy and Your Narrator ride by the name, "The Idiot Twins.") If Your Narrator has succeeded, the reader will understand that Jimmy is exactly the kind of person that will take Your Narrator surfing once a week over a summer, lending a board, leash, providing instruction and tips and even a towel, while at the same time one morning with a take-two-car strategy in place, pull out of the neighborhood so quickly that the two of us became separated and Your Narrator got lost on side streets. If this is clear, then enough is enough and no need to read number 8. If this is still a little hazy, or if you're just curious about one more AJD, then read on.

8. Jimmy texted both Dutch and me about the possibility of a guys' weekend in San Francisco in November coinciding with a Pearl Jam show. Your Narrator, a member of the PJ fan club known as the Ten Club, checked his email to see that, in a sense, Jimmy was right but, in another sense, he was wrong as the show in Nov. in SF was actually a Temple of the Dog show, which as PJ fans know consists of members of PJ and Soundgarden combined. I responded that I would look into tickets, as a fan club member with certain access privileges, and that the show was not PJ but in fact Temple of the Dog. Just saying. (I use this phrase, too, as it has the quality of the perfect little lemon squirt of a sentence to spray in the other's eye when in the right and one can't help but add one more eensy sentence that in effect doesn't add anything at all.) This is where the difficulties began as the PJ fan club ticket drawing would only permit two tickets per

fan. So assuming SFCA (San Francisco Chicagoan A) could join Dutch and Jimmy and me, that still meant that two out of Jimmy or Dutch or SFCA would have to purchase tickets when they went on sale to the general public a week after the drawing. So SFCA was contacted and signed on, and Jimmy was all set to buy the second set of two tickets. Well, lo and behold, when the tickets went on sale he couldn't seem to get any, but in the midst of the process they added another SF Temple of the Dog show the very next night, which Jimmy promptly bought four tickets to and texted the group with the news, to which Dutch replied with a three letter response: AJD. Which set off a stream of texts between Jimmy, Dutch, and me, all with SFCA receiving the stream but not chiming in once, sort of a silent witness to three old men bickering; Jimmy pushing back, saying at least he's doing something to kick-start the elusive and forever-procrastinated Guys' Weekend, taking direct aim at Dutch on this one; me trying to compliment Jimmy for the initiative but also ridicule him for his impetuousness and his inability to see his own flawed logic, really trying to be sincere on both parts and then also trying to make fun of myself for such a complicated thing to get across in a text; Jimmy telling me to sell my Ten Club tickets; me responding that it's complicated because of strict and extensive Ten Club rules like that I have to go to will call to pick up the tickets; Jimmy now going the extra Walter Sobchakian mile by texting Douggie Fresh, a successful working member of the ticket industry, who responded tersely with the info that a) Ten Club tix have to be picked up at will call so he can't sell them (obvi), and b) he prefers to do ticket business—even with friends—over email and not text on his personal cell. The text stream got as heated as a text stream between three lifelong friends can get, mainly with Jimmy suggesting that the four of us attend both shows, which is ridiculous for a variety of reasons but mainly that Temple of the Dog has a grand total of one (1) (!) studio album, and the set lists for the two shows predictably will have little variation. Meanwhile my one-year-old blew out a diaper with a state of matter—akin to this paragraph—nowhere near the ballpark of solid while I held her, and so my white shirt suddenly had like a brown map of Mexico on it, and I had to do all the cleanup and everything, so that when I got back on the stream Jimmy had ended it as abruptly as it had started with, "OK will get two for the Friday show and sell my 4 for Sat."

Rosati's at 530; plop fest 2016 at 7am the next morning

At times, Your Narrator has felt out of place in San Diego. The lack of seasons, the abundant sunlight, palm trees, flowers blooming in February. First world problems of the nth degree. Jimmy, apparently, doesn't share this feeling.

"Sometimes I just need some weather besides seventy and sunny. Just for a change." I said. "Doesn't it ever bother you, just a little, the monotony of absurdly perfect weather?"

"Fuck no."

Just had a muddy shit from a hopoverload craftie
Craft draft= back draft
Hoptober Fest= Ploppy Mess
IPA= rusty asshole!

As I have mentioned, Jimmy and I have been through a lot of life together: losing parents, starting college, being twenty-something in Chicago, finding careers, serving as one another's best man, and now having kids and being dads.

Our lives were forked when I moved out to California. It was like when I went to Ecuador for a summer, and I said goodbye to him one summer afternoon in our Lincoln Park apartment. The windows faced west and were shaded by the full, bright green of summer leaves, so that in the afternoon a diffuse green sunlight streamed into the second-floor apartment. I had my bag all packed. He was typing his dissertation on his computer, which he was always doing, and he stopped and stood up and said goodbye in the green sunlight. His eyes said, "Yeah, being a skinny, white, six-foot-four American, you'll stick out like a sore thumb. Your chances of being kidnapped and murdered are not zero." But what he *said* was: "Have fun, man. See you in a few months."

It was similar when I moved to California, except we had separate apartments and instead of one slightly surreal goodbye, there were four, maybe five, Tim-going-to-California parties with Dutch. Each time it got funnier, that I was having another going away party. So that by the time I had my real, seriously, last night out before going away, it was so funny that we had had so many going away parties that it was never really that sad.

But then two years later Jimmy had an interview at the VA in San Diego for the clinical rotation years of his PhD. Jimmy has been called Dr. since long before he earned a doctorate in psychology, but this has more to do with the movie *Fletch* than it does his study habits or stated life goals. Rather, in our twenties Jimmy made the decision to earn a PhD in psychology. "I'm going to be a suit-wearing professional one day," is what he said, or something of the sort, and even though he doesn't wear suits to work he is now indeed a professional.

He didn't expect to place at the VA in SD. His top three choices were all in Chicago. But life is funny. Two days after he gave the best man speech at my wedding, he ended up interviewing at the VA and a few months later, *voilà*, he was moving to San Diego. I found his first apartment for him in La Jolla.

The rest is history. Jimmy finished his PhD, learned to surf, and now we are both raising kids in Southern California. And in many ways, it is like he is just down the hall—except it's an interstate, the 5. But he's right there, like I can look down out of my room and he will be typing away on his computer.

Jimmy doesn't work for the VA anymore. Now he works in a private neurology clinic. But he worked at the VA for several years after finishing his rotation. And that is what makes Jimmy an interesting character study: that he routinely has debacles like refusing to come in from surfing while Dutch is waiting for him and Dutch needs to get to his MBA class at SDSU, but Jimmy can't leave in the middle of the set and doesn't even know that Dutch is fuming, and then in the afternoon he will be talking with a vet about PTSD and Iraq. That's Jimmy for you.

Just took my 2ⁿᵈ muddy dump
Worst bathroom situation in Oceanside at my work
Just awful

Sometimes systems don't work the way they are supposed to. They have glitches or errors or straight-up malfunctions. Like technology and computers: An operating system won't work, a communications system is down, someone hacks into someone else's secure system. It happens in our criminal justice system: Innocent people go to jail and guilty people go free. Sometimes they are broken, like our political $y$tem.

Our immigration system. Or our healthcare system—maybe it's getting better. I don't really know. There's the United States educational system that I am a cog in. Sometimes I (it) leave(s) children behind. And finally, there's Jimmy's favorite, the digestive system. Recently, I had the stomach flu. Food went the wrong way. It went opposite the designed direction of the system. Lying on my bathroom floor, I thought, "Jimmy was wrong. Pooping isn't the antithesis of eating—puking is."

And then sometimes systems are broken but still work in a new, unusual, and profoundly interesting and unique way. Which is what Jimmy and I learned on this particular evening.

Just took my 2nd deuce of the day and it's not even 7am

ABSORPTION

The food arrived as the third quarter got underway. With mastication, conversation dwindled and became sparse.

What was the consensus regarding the food?

The deep dish was good, but not in comparison to Chicago's deep dish. Really, it was like comparing apples and oranges. There's truly no comparison for any San Diego Chicago-style pizza. The Italian Beef, however, earned strong marks.

What happened next?

Inevitably, with Jimmy, the discussion turned to how this meal would progress through our respective digestive systems. It was at this point that SDCB announced that he hasn't passed solid waste in over twenty years. Pin-drop silence followed, at our table that is.

Fifty percent of the human bolus wanted to know: What do you mean? (SDCA was already aware of the anomaly).

It was then explained by SDCB to Dr. Jimmy and Your Narrator that SDCB lacks a colon in his digestive tract. He had it removed in high school, he explained with abundant good nature (almost as if he was telling a story of how he didn't get shotgun on a long ride) due to a reaction in his body from Accutane, an acne cream. He developed ulcerative colitis and eventually had to have a colectomy, or removal of his colon. He spent many years, including his binge-drinking college years, with an external ostomy appliance (bag). He no longer wears the appliance (bag), because of a procedure he had in his early twenties where a surgeon attached a loose pouch from his small bowel to his anal sphincter muscle.

Jimmy's eyebrows betrayed him: he was flabbergasted.

At this point, had all the food been eaten?

Most of it, yet one piece of deep dish remained that Your Narrator subsequently consumed.

While Your Narrator consumed the last slice of deep dish, what other things did SDCB share regarding his unique situation?

Amazingly, SDCB still enjoyed a relatively normal undergraduate college experience, including alcohol and sexual forays. SDCB shared some of these mostly zany and funny-when-looking-back-on-it episodes. For example, once he passed out with a girl in his bed, and his roommate found his emptied bag lying in the bathroom. The roommate realized the danger of having a girl in the bed while being bagless and rushed in to wake him up and replace the bag. Another story involved him filling his bag while simultaneously receiving oral sex.

Jimmy literally couldn't believe it.

Questions followed about dietary needs, pragmatic day-to-day living, and general what's-it- like-to-live-without-a-colon questions. SDCB answered them all very comfortably and good-naturedly, even the one about the class action lawsuit (which he has received no compensation from).

What happened next?

Jimmy sneezed.

How did SDCA and SDCB react?

Initially with mild alarm and concern. Secondly with interest and curiosity. Thirdly with mirth.

A link to 35 photos of signs that are literally toilet humor (Including NO LAUGHING AT OTHER PEOPLE'S FARTS, PLEASE DO NOT WIPE YOUR DISGUSTING BOOGERS ON THE WALL YOU ARE GROWN MEN THIS ISN'T KINDERGARTEN, (handwritten) THE GARBAGE CAN IS NOT A TOILET!!!, PLEASE KEEP POOP GRUNTS AND OTHER NOISES TO A REASONABLE VOLUME)

At this time Your Narrator feels it is appropriate to address potential critics who might find this entire literary bolus crude, sophomoric, an exorbitant waste of time, or somehow beneath either a) Your Narrator, or b) anyone reading the entire bolus from lips to anus.

Your Narrator feels strongly that a writer, and particularly an aspiring humorist, must take risks, and that the potential gains outweigh the anticipated losses in readership for the following reasons:

1. Digestion unites all humans. From world leaders to the people cleaning their bathrooms, all humans eat, digest, defecate, suffer indigestion, vomit, pass gas, and experience borborygmi.
2. We can all use a break from the seriousness of Life.
3. It is often necessary to challenge convention of decorum and appropriateness.

4. Your Narrator sees a similarity between food and experience as they pass ineluctably through humans.
   a. Both start outside the body and pass through the body.
   b. Both have a useless portion that is expelled, a useful portion that is needed, and a harmful portion that, if kept and absorbed into the body, causes illness and potentially death.
   c. Both have various taste qualities of good, bad, bland, flavorful, memorable, and forgettable.
   d. Your Narrator wishes to remember the experience of one night, to hold it to the light, to enhance and examine and crystallize it for the future, as so many days and nights slip past unexamined in the frantic speed of living.
5. Dr. Jimmy is a character of contradictions and complexities, and friendship is a subject worth writing about and narrating and bringing to life on the page. While this life on the page does not meet the standard of a Lear or Hamlet, it is not through any fault of Dr. Jimmy's, but that of Your Narrator.
6. This essay presented an opportunity to weave in the ineluctable necessity of belonging to systems. That society and life is one unfathomable mysterious system, one that fascinates Jimmy despite his eternal lightness of being; that time passes, crazy shit happens, Death and Taxes, on small scales and large: galaxies swirl and worlds begin and end eternally, that it's all squeezed out at the end, so we might as well have a good laugh while going down.
7. Sometimes systems fail or contain anomalies.
8. Writing should be fun, at least some of the time.

Taking a huge shit

Here's a quick stab at writing as fun. One Sunday at brunch Jimmy told me he felt remorse about a comment he made to Dutch's girlfriend Whitney. Jimmy was commenting on how good the goop was on his eggs Benedict.

"This is some good goop!"

Whitney, a foodie and career server, was clearly miffed that he would refer to hollandaise sauce as "goop." Jimmy, now miffed himself, said, "Oh, sorry, guess that's not the right thing to say. Is there an industry term for goop?"

Whitney rolled her eyes.

"I think it's sauce," I said.

Anyway, we've always laughed about that exchange and rehashed that line a bunch: "Is there an industry term for goop?" But then recently Jimmy said he felt bad about it.

He explained, "By making a joke about the sauce, I was putting down her profession, and thus putting down her as a person. I was belittling her."

I had never seen it that way, but now I did. "I could see that," I said. Then Jimmy said something that I believe to be a cornerstone of him as an individual.

"I'm not sure I believe in God, but I believe in being nice to people."

STILL WINDING THROUGH THE INTESTINES

We were in his front room. Jimmy's wife, Gloria, was holding my daughter. All the other kids were playing. I thought back to when we were freshmen at Indiana and there was this girl, a RedStepper, who mayhap perchance might have sort of liked me. She was hot. Smitty, from Connecticut. I could make her laugh like *that*. It was just easy for some reason. I was always making her laugh, and we would flirt in that freshmen, just-arrived-at-school kind of way. But, to put it mildly, girls weren't exactly my strong suit. And Jimmy knew this. One day we were smoking pot at Brandon's house off campus out of his small wooden bowl. His house was kind of a refuge for Jimmy and me since Brandon grew up with us in Riverview. We would go there to get away from the overwhelming reality of everything being so new, to feel some familiarity. Well, on this particular afternoon we got pretty stoned. And, I'm not sure if this really happened, or if it's only how I remembered it, but I think Jimmy called up Smitty and then handed me the phone, just to see me get all Botchy Botcherson because he knew I got all tight and nervous talking to girls when I was stoned. In my memory I see him, higher than a bat's ass and enjoying the debacle, watching me fumble and squirm for words. Maybe he was jealous because Smitty was hot. Or maybe he was mad that I had made fun of him by calling a girl he had made out with "Baba O'Riley." Or maybe it was the general, callous, and typical groupthink-teenage-meanness-cruelty we all showed each other in high school. Or maybe I called Smitty without even knowing I did. Maybe (in Keith Richards growl) *it was just my imagination. . .* Either way, I think she acted differently around me after that, like she suspected that maybe I had some deeper problems.

And here I was, sitting on Jimmy's couch twenty years later, with our kids playing all around us. I was about to bring it up, to verify if indeed he did call Smitty, but I didn't. I wasn't so sure. Plus, I didn't want to have to tell the whole story with all the context and background. Besides, Gloria already knew about the time Jimmy made out drunk one night with a girl, appropriately named Tyranny, that I was seriously hung up on for most of junior year. I remember I didn't talk to him before I left for my study abroad program that summer. The old cold shoulder. He called me the night before I left, but I didn't answer. I sat in the kitchen and listened to his message on my dad's answering machine. "Dude…Sorry…Call me…"

We hashed it out, though. That and a dozen other botches, like the time I gave both him and his computer a virus right before some big deadline in his PhD program. In a weird way, those things made our friendship stronger.

"Dick move," Gloria had said about Tyranny.

been constipated bc I'm on this low carb diet. Tryna lose weight for a insurance exam. Was so constipated. Ate a bag of spinach last night. Took a 4 ft shit today.

No joke.

Worst spelling pooo of my life

Smelling…hahah the irony

THE ANUS

The colon talk died down and the game heated up. With the season on the ropes, Aaron Rodgers converted a 4th and 20 from the team's own end zone with a 60-yard answered prayer of a heave to Jeff Janis. A second prayer, known as a Hail Mary, this one a 41-yard connection to Janis, sent the game to overtime, much to the delight and amazement of the packed stadium along with the sparsely filled restaurant. Then to open OT Carson Palmer connected with Larry Fitzgerald for a 75-yard pass play, bringing the Chicago Cardinals all the way to the 5-yard line, which is where Fitzgerald scored from two plays later, ending the season of the rival Green Bay

Packers and sending the San Diego Chicago Cardinal fans home happy.

I'm crudding now

The intriguing part, the anomaly, is what happened to start OT. The referee, Clete Blakeman, flipped a coin that never flipped, literally staying "flat as a pancake." The Packers lost the toss, but complained about the flat-as-a-pancake coin, so the referee Blakeman decided to re-toss the coin. This is not in the NFL rulebook—there is nothing in the book about a flipless flip. Cue league statement of implacable neutrality:

"The referee used his judgement to determine that basic fairness dictated that the coin should flip for the toss to be valid. That is why he re-tossed the coin."

Here's where it gets interesting. When Blakeman flipped it a second time, he didn't ask Rodgers to call it a second time. He assumed Rodgers would stay with his original call of tails.

Rodgers called the flip a debacle. Here's his quote after the game: "Clete had it on heads. He was showing heads. So I called tails. And it didn't flip," Rodgers said. "It just tossed up in the air and did not turn over at all. It just landed on the ground. So obviously that was not right. He picked the coin up and flipped it to tails, and then he flipped it without giving me a chance to give me a re-call there. It was confusing. I think he was trying to avoid the embarrassment of what happened—he flipped it quickly."

And here's CBS sportswriter John Breech with a conclusion: "Although the Cardinals won the toss both times, Rodgers' point is that maybe they wouldn't have won it the second time if he had been given a chance to make a heads or tails call. Rodgers based his first call on how Blakeman was holding the coin. Either way, the Packers lost the toss both times and the Cardinals went on to win the game by scoring a touchdown on their first offensive possession."

Sometimes it feels like day-in, day-out, life is One Big Coin Toss and things tend to even out over time. But sometimes the coin doesn't flip. And what do you do? Do you re-flip? If the coin is re-flipped, do you change your initial answer? What if you never get the chance? What then, what then?

That is what I wondered as I drove home, that and how SDCB's digestive tract would handle the craft beers, "the Chief" Italian Beef sandwich, the deep-dish sausage pizza, and the fried mushrooms the next day.

HISTORIC(!) RUGBY

Everybody loves a story.
—William Zinsser in "Writing to Learn"

Gather around friends and let me tell you a tale, the tale of historic Rugby, Tennessee. It all starts with an Englishman named Thomas Hughes, born in 1822 somewhere in England that ends in *-shire*. Thomas, known in this story hencewith as the Tomster, goes to this prominent, progressive school called the Rugby School, in Rugby— somewhere else in England that also ends in *-shire*.

Then in 1857, the Tomster writes a book about his experience called *Tom Brown's School Days* which becomes something of a classic, ushers in an entire British school genre, becomes a big textbook in Japan, and even inspires the Harry Potter series, if you can believe it. The book, in a nutshell, "espouses the ideals of Christian socialism." It's all about what the Tomster feels is the ideal way to develop boys into men that will make for a good society for all—a real page-turner.

A big influence on the Tomster was his headmaster at Rugby, one Dr. Thomas Arnold. This guy, henceforth known as Dr. T-Bone, was a religious zealot who based his educational system on classical languages. One interesting thing about

Dr. T-Bone is that he turned his back on physical science and wrote, basically, that he would rather his son think the sun goes round the Earth and that the stars are a bunch of spangles, as long as he is straight on Christian moral and political philosophy. Dr. T-Bone had three primary objectives, in this presumably very rigid order: 1) cure of the soul; 2) moral development; and 3) intellectual development. It's fair to say that number three was probably something of a distant third.

Dr. T-Bone had a big influence on education all over England, resulting in a bunch of schools adopting his structure and ideals. He may have had a lot to do with sport, like cricket, becoming a big part of schools, but this is a tad ambiguous.

Anyway, the Tomster is clearly a big fan of Dr. T-Bone and really buys into his whole philosophy regarding Christian values and morals, and he latches on to the idea of cooperative ownership of community businesses.

As the 1860's get underway, the Tomster is a world-famous author and English gentleman and has a bunch of author-writer friends. One of whom is this poet James Russell Lowell, henceforwithal known as Lowball. Lowball is a Harvard grad, a Romantic poet, and part of a group of New England Poets called the Fireside Poets. These bards earned this name, presumably, because you can read their poems to your family right at the— you guessed it—fireside. (This group managed to set itself apart from the other poetry and poets' groups of the era: the higher-quality and longer-lasting, but ultimately more costly poetry of the Beeswaxcandleside Poets; the cheaper, quicker, and unpleasant-smelling Animalfatcandleside Poets—often read near mirrors to double their weak and loose meanings; the portable, racy, and erotic bedroom-reading specialists known as the Chamberstickside Poets; and the bourgeois, snooty, and ornate poems of the Candelabraside Poets.)

Lowball is kind of a big deal. Beyond abolitionist poetry, he earns a law degree from Harvard and becomes a critic, an editor, and even a diplomat to Spain. Lowball writes a lot of satire of critics, including something called *The Biglow Papers*, which depicts the Yankee dialect and is maybe the first time that a writer actually writes like people talked, which influences Mark Twain and H.L. Mencken. So yeah, kind of a big deal.

The Tomster goes to Boston in 1870 to visit Lowball and they start talking. The Tomster tells Lowball about this system in England called primogeniture. Lowball says, "Primo-what?" And the Tomster says, "Exactly." So they have a good laugh, but then the Tomster gets going in earnest about primo-what, which he explains is this tradition of the oldest son inheriting everything, and the second, third and so on getting nada, zilch, squat, diddly or however you say nothing in 1870s slang. These second and third sons, the Tomster goes on to explain, end up jobless and idle and sort of like a blight on society—the exact opposite of what Dr. T-Bone envisioned for young men. Their very souls are in trouble, the Tomster says.

Long before Joseph Heller came along, the Tomster likely struggled for the right words to explain the *Catch-22* situation: The second and third sons are too proud to do the low-paying but honest jobs that are available, and there simply aren't enough of the bourgeois, high-paying jobs that, in their own estimation, aren't beneath them. And meanwhile the first son gets everything and lives high and mighty over it all, for a while anyway. The economy, the Tomster confides, isn't helping either. In fact, it's as much a source of the problem as is the primo-what. It's just a mess, the Tomster says to Lowball over some chowda.

Well, Lowball asks the Tomster if he has heard of the Boston-based Board of Aid to Land Ownership, which helps unemployed urban craftsman relocate to rural areas. No, the Tomster confesses, he has not heard of this program, but immediately you can imagine his Dr. T-Bone inspired gears immediately get a-grinding.

So the Tomster goes back to England and writes this in response to criticism that *Tom Brown's School Days* is too preachy:

> *Why, my whole object in writing at all was to get the chance of preaching! When a man comes to my time of life and has his bread to make, and very little time to spare, is it likely that he will spend almost the whole of his yearly vacation in writing a story just to amuse people? I think not. At any rate, I wouldn't do so myself.*
>
> *— Thomas Hughes, preface to the sixth edition of Tom Brown's School Days*

(It should be noted that the Tomster wrote a sequel, *Tom Brown at Oxford*, in 1861 that basically flopped.)

Then in 1878, the Board of Aid President Franklin Webster Smith, hencewithforthcoming known as Smitty, travels to the Cumberland Plateau with an agent from the Cincinnati Southern Railway Co., Cyrus Clarke, a.k.a. Clarkels. They are impressed with its "virgin forests, clear air, and scenic gorges."

So Smitty goes back to Boston, but the conditions there are better: A lot of the urban craftsman don't need relocating. So Smitty calls Lowball who calls the Tomster and *voilà* the Tomster buys the land the Board of Aid offers near the Cumberland Plateau and calls it Rugby, fittingly, after his sentimental and halcyon school days.

Here's where it gets all rubber-meets-the-road social science experiment. The Tomster starts recruiting these primo-what drunk degenerate second and third sons to come to this pristine Tennessee forest. Smitty lays out the town, choosing an area that looks like a resort even though it's seven miles from the nearest railroad stop.

The first wave of settlers comes out to Rugby around the late 1870s; they start erecting structures like the three-story Tabard Inn which is straight out of a Capote or F.Scott Fitzgerald novel: very aristocratic and ghostly with lawns for croquet and tennis—right in the middle of the Tennessee wilderness.

They hold a grand opening for the town in October of 1880 and the Tomster himself comes all the way from England. (It's interesting to speculate here exactly how long it took this wave of immigrants and the Tomster to travel, but I would estimate it was at least two weeks and maybe as long as a month. From what I can tell, it seems like with a steel ship and steam engine they were able to cross the Atlantic in something like seven days by the 1880s. And the railways were getting faster, too, but it still maybe took a week to get all the way out to the wilderness in between Nashville and Knoxville, even if you traveled—as I assume the Tomster did—first class.)

So the Tomster arrives and lays out his plans for an anti-materialistic, utopian Rugby in what must have been, for lack of a better term, a doozy of a speech.

I like to imagine him getting up to speak on a fresh October morn, resplendent with the beauty of changing leaves, crisp air, mild, pleasant breezes, and the overall magic autumnal wonder that dazzles with golden warmth. When I close my eyes, I can picture it:

The Tomster steps up in the bright sunshine against the impossibly bright blue sky and tells the settlers that everyone will have to pay five dollars, like a tax, to be part of the public commissary, "thus ensuring public ownership." He then goes on (and on) about guaranteed personal liberty and some real savory Dr. T-Bonian moralistic and political nuggets. A real sort of rah-rah, pep-rally, together-we-stand, divided-we-fall, all-for-one kind of speech, loaded like a baked potato with lots of Christian and moral preachy stuff, which he had at least a month to revise and tinker with on the trip that he makes *without* his wife or any of his nine children. (His wife basically wanted NOTHING, like zip, to do with Rugby.) He tells the mostly secular, alcoholic immigrants about the Episcopal Church and stresses that the church they will be too hungover to attend can be used for any denomination.

I can picture the settlers, too: a crowd of second and third sons basically on something akin to a vacation in a resort-like pristine wilderness, nodding politely through it all. I see them smiling and winking right through the parts about self-betterment, the Christian servant and productive gentleman of society, the arts and sports and library—except at the end of the speech, which hits them like a frying pan to the face, when the Tomster says, very clearly and in no way mincing words, "No. Booze."

I reckon he loses them then and there. Superficially, he probably lost them pretty early on with his preaching, but they were willing to grin and bear it for form's sake because they could go back to sipping moonshine at the Gentleman's Swimming Hole once this author guy finally shuts his trap, but at this last moralistic jab, he surely loses them for good.

So this English Victorian village social experiment is now growing right in the heart of post-Civil War Dixie wilderness. All these newspapers like the *New York Times* and magazines like *Harper's* are following it, probably somewhat skeptically. In London, too, there is lots of interest and coverage from the media. After all, the Tomster is not just a famous author but also a lawyer, a member of Parliament, and a judge.

And how does it do? What happens? At first, thanks to the beauty and resort-like surroundings, pretty well.

According to author and historian Brian Stagg's book (which might make for an entertaining *Wheel of Fortune* puzzle with vowels galore) *Distant Eden: Tennessee's Rugby Colony: a History of the English Colony at Rugby, Tennessee, with a Guide to the Remaining Original Buildings,* "By 1884, the colony boasted over four hundred residents (including the Tomster's mom), sixty-five framed public buildings and houses, a tennis team, a social club, and a literary and dramatic society. In 1885, Rugby established a university, Arnold School, named for Rugby School headmaster Thomas Arnold."

Another interesting thing about the Tomster is that he establishes this library that still stands today. They build it in 1882 and arranged for some Boston bookseller, maybe someone Lowball knew or something, to provide the books— some seven thousand. (When you visit the library, you are not allowed to touch the books, some of them dating back to the seventeenth century, so it has this sad, frozen-in-time quality, interesting and worth preserving but also tragic in the sense that the words and knowledge are forever trapped inside and doomed to the darkness of their own closed covers. Not a place that any living author would aspire to be. Sort of like in the movie *Good Will Hunting,* when Will tells Sean about his friends Shakespeare and Nietzsche, and Sean responds, "Well that's great. They're all dead." I imagine him saying the same thing visiting this stuffy old dusty one-room library where they don't even open the windows. "That's great, Rugby. But these books are all dead.")

Early on, the Tomster's experiment is going well. The degenerate English guys have escaped a Dickensian industrial that include strict adherence to Christian morals and basically sober living.

People starve. The town struggles and declines. In 1884 the Tabard Inn, veering into Faulkner short story territory, burns to the ground. In 1887, the Tomster's mom dies and is buried in Rugby. *The Rugbeian* ceases publication. After his mom passes, the Tomster never returns to Rugby. (One can probably infer here that the Tomster's mom and his wife were not very close. In fact, it's interesting to speculate why the Tomster's mom chose to move to Rugby at the age of 83, away from all her grandchildren.) By the end of 1887, all of the original colonists are gone.

Five years later, one of the Tomster's lawyers and partners named Sir Henry, hencewith known as Sir Hank, comes and reorganizes the Board of Aid and tries to harvest the area's natural resources— essentially the antithesis of the anti-materialistic vision of the Tomster. But Sir Hank doesn't fare much better with the lack of a workforce with any sort of appetite for actual work.

The entire story of Rugby would be lost along with the ashes of the Tabard Inn if it wasn't for the son of Robert Walton, forthhencewith known as Little Bobby. His dad, Robert Walton (a.k.a. Big Bob), was the Cincinnati engineer who the Tomster and his Brit lawyer buddies put in charge of the colony in 1882, right when it started going a little south after the media-labeled epidemic of seven typhoid deaths. Big Bob does his darndest trying, among other things, to open a tomato cannery operation, which fails, once again because of the poor soil and poor work ethic of the colonists.

Little Bobby is basically a child of the dying town. Once he grows up, he makes it his life mission to preserve its history. He protects and maintains some of the buildings, like the

1880's urban jobless *Catch-22* misery for these rugged woods and serene streams and beautiful mountains. They're stoked.

And then life happens. First, an "epidemic" of typhoid hits the town, claiming seven people, including the editor of Rugby's newspaper, *the Rugbeian*. Though only seven people die, the press and the media are the real killer, as the whole reason to visit Rugby is its resort-like qualities, and who exactly wants to visit a place with typhoid in the headlines?

The Tabard Inn has to close, and there's no one but ghosts of upper-class tourists playing croquet on the overgrown grasses. Tourism takes a hit, but also the Tomster over across the pond isn't exactly scrutinizing the details of his experiment.

Mainly, the Appalachian natives didn't trust this Ohio railway agent Clarkels—not a surprise there—with all his options on land. So a bunch of these Appalachian folks, probably safe to say not big readers (despite the library), refuse to sell or file lawsuits and it all drags on and basically becomes one big headache for the regular old Winston Berkshire the Third, who is just trying to buy a little land and maybe have a cabin of his own to pass out in.

Besides the whole Clarkels land ownership debacle, there's also the very real and T-Bone-scorned physical science fact of the poor soil that Smitty chose to build Rugby on. And despite its resort-like qualities that no one will patronize after all the typhoid headlines, *the Rugbeian* can't even defend or promote the town's own tourism because the editor himself succumbed.

But the real downfall, the nail in the coffin if you will, is that these English gent-colonists are not what you would call workers. They are, in fact, the opposite: lazy drinkers. And the Tomster, visiting once for about a month, probably in summer and staying in the Kingstone Lisle or the Newbury House (nice digs indeed), isn't exactly motivating them with his speeches library and the church and the Newbury house, until the 1940s, when the timber companies start to really devour the virgin forests in earnest and the federal government steps in to help preserve a slice of history.

In the 1960s, they form the nonprofit group Historic Rugby so that, just as my dad, sister, uncle, and I did one Sunday, you too can take a drive out to the country and, as the website claims, find "both exciting AND relaxing things to do!"

The Video. Begin your visit with the short twenty-two-minute national award-winning historical video *The Power of a Dream* (free of charge!) in the "comfortable" Johnson Theatre. (The name of the award is not clear.)

The Tour. For $7 each ($6 for seniors over 60, $4 for students K-12, and free for preschoolers), you can take the very same tour we did that leads through the Thomas Hughes Free Public Library (over 7,000 untouchable volumes), the 1884 Kingston Lisle Founder's Home (including an old stove, furniture, and a piano that you *can* sit down and play), the one-room schoolhouse (built in 1906 after a fire destroyed the original building), and the 1887 Christ Church Episcopal (with its original furnishings, light fixtures, and rosewood organ), which still has services on Sundays.

Free to Roam. After visiting the church, if you spent any time at all sitting in the pews, you'll want to stretch your legs and ease that pain in your lower back by heading down to the Rugby Printing Press. With its original equipment and machinery, a volunteer will print your name on a bookmark that readers and possessive children under eleven will really relish. Then, like us, why not head over and grab some shepherd's pie at the Harrow Road Café (built in 1980)? It's a bit heavy, so afterward you'll want to walk down to the Gentleman's Swimming Hole, where so many immigrants avoided back-breaking manual labor. You'll walk right past a cluster of trees and bushes where the Tabard Inn once stood. After wading in the cool waters of the Gentlemen's Swimming Pool (be sure to check for ticks; my dad found two after visiting), you can head to the old cemetery and, unlike her inconsiderate, ungrateful daughter-in-law, pay your respects to the Tomster's mom, who was buried there in 1887.

Much of the area surrounding Rugby, which originally attracted Clarkels and Smitty and the Tomster himself, is now state forest, national park, and recreation areas. If you still have the energy, you can take a hike and contemplate the buildings and croquet ghosts and scattered hardy residents that have preserved a life that lives, on and on, through the years, like the books, untouched by time or tourist. If you can whistle, I recommend "Ob-La-Di Ob-La-Da."

Because life goes on, except in Rugby.

SOS IN THE JURY LOUNGE 2

Summoned Again

Here's the conversation between bailiffs as I enter:

"You know he's eating lunch with the captain over there?"

"Is he?"

"Yeah, you know how it goes. Once you get into administration you get sucked into the whole. . ."

The other bailiff didn't interrupt him, he just stopped speaking.

"Oh, I know."

"That's the captain who saved him. If it wasn't for him, he'd be downtown."

7:57. Here I am again. Back in the J Lounge. Most of the seats face east. But I am facing south in a small section in the northwest corner of the room. I wanted a table, but I was running late thanks to a wrong turn. I thought the Civic Center exit would take me to the court system. Nope. I had to turn around and have my phone navigate me through the back roads of Vista, listening to Kings of Leon's "The Bucket," sleep-deprived, feeling the old irritation of sitting at red lights when you are in a hurry.

But I made it. Right on time. I wanted a seat to observe people unobtrusively. I partly accomplished that goal, although I still have to be careful and not too obvious if they look up— being observed not only creeps people out but changes their behavior and keeps the good stuff well-guarded.

Here comes a judge. Good morning. Orientation. His primary desire is to say, "thank you." Without us, the system doesn't work.

It is the same judge as last year.

The film. I have a very poor angle from which to view it. The east-facing audience has a direct view. My angle is probably something close to fifteen degrees. Right as the film starts, a woman walks in late and sits down directly in my line of view.

It's the same video as last year.

I am feeling a tinge of anxiety because of the sign: NO CHECK-IN REQUIRED. My anxiety stems from the following two questions: How do they know I'm here? How can they call me so that I receive "credit" for being here?

I rise to affirm the NO CHECK-IN REQUIRED policy, but the line at the desk is too long. I go back to look at the sign. Not only is it in ALL CAPS, but it is highlighted.

8:23. The video is still going. I'm thinking they'll come around and collect the forms. I think I remember that now. Why don't they do that at the beginning? There is a bar code. Can't they scan us as we enter?

8:26. The video ends.

"Academy Award-winning stuff, huh?" says the clerk. I feel like she said that last year. Maybe not. She rides to and from the podium in a cart.

"You know you want that huge check," she says, telling us to make sure the address is correct on or form.

We all make choices for how to pass the time. For example, a woman in a black jacket is reading *People* magazine. The woman behind her, older, with a colorful pink floral jacket, is reading *Hamlet*. I pull out my notebook and start a-jotting.

8:28. The woman reading *People* gets up and is standing in line at the counter that runs along the western wall.

We sign and date the forms and tear off the perforated portion. They ask us to write our phone numbers down.

"To receive credit, pass your forms to the left." I feel validated that she uses the word "credit."

The forms are passed to the left, toward me. The rivers of forms flow down the rows; I receive the piles and pass them to the person on my left. We are like the ocean in our little section.

"Feel free to throw darts at your timesheet, or set it on fire," the clerk says about the timesheets at the back that you can get for your employer. It is her third attempt at humor and she is only getting polite smiles.

8:36. The clerk is still speaking. There are eleven rows of seats in the main section, which has four aisles. Each row has twenty-eight seats, four groups of seven. My little side section has four rows of five seats, like a theater box on the side of a stage. Our seats have more cushioning. Our section is right next to the Quiet Area, which is next to an area of tables and then the entrance.

". . . So you won't have to endure the horrible California weather to get to that courtroom." It is her fifth attempt at humor. (The fourth was something about the bailiff carrying you out kicking and screaming.)

The woman reading *People* has left. Another woman, who came in late, while I was standing in line having my mini-panic attack, walked in front of me, very, very slowly, on the way to her seat.

8:41. Break. I leave my stuff (including my bag containing my laptop), grab a magazine from the top of the magazine rack, the *Nation,* and walk across the J Lounge, quickly, to take a poo. The bathroom is crowded. I get the last available stall. It's a good thing, too.

8:51. In the bathroom, I read the editor's letter from the September 2017 issue. The letter is entitled, "Climate Denialism Kills." It is all about Hurricane Harvey and some other international storms that haven't received as much news coverage. Then the article moves into Trump's policies and the people he has appointed to lead various organizations, like the EPA and NASA, who don't have scientific backgrounds. Also all his coals and oil policies. The writer claims that Trump is killing millions of people with his policies. That would be some trial.

9:00 Yeah! No one stole my computer while I was pooping. I am estimating that the room is 60 percent full. Most of the people are in the back. All the tables and the Quiet Area are full. If the J Lounge was a man's head, his hairline would be receding and the hair on top of his head would be thinning. The average age might be something like forty-nine, maybe older. As I glance along the rows, there seems to be an equal ratio of men to women.

The woman directly in front of me, doing a puzzle on her phone, has her left leg crossed over her right and is rocking it rhythmically, though periodically she stops, then it starts up again. It's like she is kicking a little ball, keeping it suspended in the air.

The woman blocking my view of the video has moved. She is now behind me. A Hispanic man is now in her seat, blue jeans, blue shirt, blue hat. He's reading a *People* that he snagged from the magazine rack. Presently he finishes and goes back to the rack for another rag. The slow walker, the one who took the seat of the other *People* magazine reader who has now left, is reading a black book without a jacket. I can't read the title, but

I think the author is Dave Shack, though I can't quite make out all those letters, either. She is holding it close to her eyes. The woman with the pink flowered jacket is back into *Hamlet*. It looks like she started on *Act I, Scene I.* I'm guessing it's not the first time she's read it.

Everyone is either reading or on a device. A few newspapers dot the crowd. There is a low murmur of voices and shuffling feet and bodies and coughs and throat-clearing. The ceiling has eight rows of fluorescent lights. Each row has seven lights. The carpet is clean and I don't see any stains. Someone has vacuumed recently and removed the garbage. To my left, along the east wall and just north of the magazine and book rack, are two garbage cans and a recycling bin.

Blue is flipping through his new mag. I can't see what it is, but the pages aren't grabbing or holding his attention. Behind him, Kick is still kicking, though the phone is now in her purse and she is just sitting, staring, thinking.

9:08. Heading to the snack bar. I leave my belongings: journal, pen, bag (with laptop), coffee cup (nicknamed El Capitán), and red water bottle, and walk west down the aisle. I pass all the tables and turn north, pass the NO CHECK-IN REQUIRED (highlighted) sign, and head out of the J Lounge. I walk over to the snack bar on the opposite wall from the metal detectors and south entrance, just before the elevators. I am briefly tempted to go with a breakfast burrito that's sitting under a heating lamp but opt for a healthier option and purchase a banana for $1.09.

I eat the banana and look out the window at the people coming and going. Then it's back to my seat and this here trusty notebook.

Blue is gone. Kick is kicking, back on her phone. Three seats down from Kick, a man is sleeping. His head is nodding in that heavy, uncomfortable way that jerks upward and stirs him momentarily before slowly sinking again. When our kids do it in the car, Megan calls it "The Nod" (a predecessor to the more extreme "Broken Neck" deep sleep). Speaking of, she texts me to tell me that Delaney, our one-year-old who was kicking me at 4:30 this morning after Megan finally relented and brought her into our bed, is "down." Hamlet has gotten up. I don't see her very pink and noticeable jacket. There is exactly one conversation going on in the J Lounge, in the back row. Everyone can hear it, though in my little boxed section between the Quiet Area and the east wall I can't quite hear the gist of what they are saying. An old guy and a young guy are both smiling a lot, nodding, and grinning at the other's comments. It seems very amiable.

9:18. Some jurors are called to the back counter. The jury officials need to "talk to them." It's like school. What needs to be discussed? Of course, the Big Drama of the day is the uncertainty hovering over all of us: Will we be chosen?

I see Blue. He is now diagonal and across from me, on the far side of the lounge. If I moved over and then back to the corner behind me, we would be as far away as it is possible for two Potential Jurors (seated, that is) to be, as the crow flies. I say seated because behind Blue is a small kitchen section with some vending machines. There is a sink and a microwave. Blue has a small coffee from the snack bar, but no magazine. I can see him perfectly through the crowd. Despite the distance, there is nothing obstructing us. You could tie a fishing line from his forehead to mine and it would bisect the J Lounge diagonally, like a sandwich.

Hamlet is back. She has a smartphone. I'm guessing she is close to seventy. She has a prominent hooked nose and one side of her gray hair is held back with a barrette. On the east wall, in between the first garbage can and the recycling bin, a young bearded man sits crossed-legged (what my teachers called Indian Style during my elementary education, but that is now generally referred to in elementary schools as Criss-Cross Applesauce—a position that currently is difficult for me to do for any length of time with my limited flexibility, despite my yoga practice). He is eating a breakfast burrito, using a small plastic ramekin to drizzle red salsa on it before taking bearded bites. He also has a bottle of juice, maybe cranberry. All his disposal and recycling needs are at arm's length. I'm having a little regret, watching him drizzle the salsa carefully, over my banana decision.

If the space near me along the east wall was a chess board, the two garbage cans would be rooks and the recycling bin would be a knight, with the spaces open between.

Down the row from the slow walker with the black book, two young men are playing a game. I can't see what it is. They appear to know each other and have planned their J service together. Everyone else is a stranger.

The Nod is awake. His attempt to nap was pointless anyway. He is scanning his phone.

The old guy and young guy in the back row are still chatting very amicably. The man sitting cross-legged on the chess board is finished with his burrito. He crumples the wrapper with the empty salsa ramekin inside it, shoves it in the bag, crumples this and throws it away in one motion, into the garbage can without a knight. His spot on the floor is probably the king's spot, though I prefer, for some reason only inanimate objects in the analogy. He still has half a bottle of juice left.

9:28. Inside the Quiet Area, maybe two feet away from me and behind a pane of glass, a man is playing a video game on his laptop. It looks like a modern version of *The Legend of Zelda*. He has a muffin wrapped tightly in cellophane. The other people around him at the tables all have laptops too and appear to be working, though you can never tell. They look like serious working adults being productive on a Tuesday morning. But then again, if I was sitting across from mid-20s-*Zelda* here, I would think he was working too, based on his expression of concentration. There's only one person in the Quiet Area not on a laptop— a guy in the corner who appears to be grading papers.

I get up to pee, walking all the way around the theater-style seating, past Blue, to the restroom. On the way I stopped by the counter, blow my nose, and pick up some extra tissue. My sinuses have been a mess lately, a real mess.

Now that I'm back in my seat I notice Kick's motion, with her right foot suspended, is entirely different. It is like a shake, like she has sand on top of her shoe that she wants to gently slide off. Shake shake shake. Still. Shake shake shake. Still. The shoes are pink canvas with a rubber sole, sort of like comfortable house shoes but not something you would want to do any serious walking in. Shake shake shake. Still. Sometimes she puts both feet on the ground and bounces her heels up and down. Then she puts the right foot back over the left. Shake shake shake. Still. She's back on her phone, playing the puzzle game again.

The two friends are playing chess. I saw it on the way back from the restroom. It's looks like some kind of speed chess, but it's not clear how much time they have for each turn or how time is factored. They keep laughing.

Blue shot me a keen look when I left the restroom. He's sitting in the same place, with his arms crossed, looking straight ahead. He could be thinking about literally anything. The diagonal line of sight between us is still clear.

The men's restroom has a diaper changing station. I can't imagine anyone bringing in their kid. So why the station?

Kick gets up and heads to the kitchen.

Near the kitchen in the last row, just north of Blue, on the other side of a large pillar where there are three seats, a woman sits on the floor. She is wearing a scarf, one of those very lightweight ones that are strictly for style points and provide essentially zero warmth. She has a Double Big Gulp soda. It's huge and about half full. I can't remember what she was doing when I walked past her, probably because my attention was drawn to the size of her beverage. If I took a pic of her, I could use it in a science class to show how organisms can find a niche in their environment, like an owl burrowed into a hole in a cactus.

Kick is back, in her seat and kicking.

Hamlet is now reading the *LA Times*, maybe from two days ago as it still has the World Series on the front page. As I'm watching, the woman one seat over from her strikes up a convo. I can't see her very well. She's behind Slow Walker Black Book and telling Hamlet-LA Times about an experience on a grand jury. Hamlet-LA Times is smiling politely and occasionally laughs. That is a good convo starter, I think. Common ground: "Have you ever served on a jury before?"

Behind the chess game (more laughter), another young man is eating a burrito. The other burrito guy is now in the front row, reading a magazine.

The old guy and young guy in the back row, center right section, are really yukking it up over there. The old guy keeps nodding and laughing. Not a lot of disagreement so far between the two. Maybe not any.

I can see the woman talking to Hamlet-LA Times. She has a kind face, like the face of a mom, sort of birdlike with glasses that don't have bottom rims. "I was born in San Diego, so it's good to be back here. I liked it there but I don't really miss it."

The convo has moved from general to personal.

We are waiting. Killing time.

9:45. I text Megan about the diaper station. The convo between the two women has moved onto Netflix and TV watching habits. HLAT asks, "So what did you in South Dakota?"

"I worked in a hospital [inaudible]. I'm retired." They are really getting along. HLAT is smiling.

I get up to stretch and walk. I head over to the kitchen. The owl nook niche woman is gone, but her Double Big Gulp is still there. Maybe she's peeing. Next to the drink on the floor is a travel guidebook to France.

On the walk back, there is another person writing. A bearded white dude with long dreads. He is also writing in a notebook, in ALL CAPS. I wonder what it's about, whom it's for? I make a joke to myself about peering over his shoulder to read it, and, when he turns, discussing capitalization rules.

Kick is gone. Nowhere to be seen.

No one else has been called.

SDak and HLAT are really getting along. SDak likes to sleep at seventy-two degrees. She likes it cool but not too cold.

I get up to look at the magazine rack. Also, to check the thermostat, inspired by SDak. It's seventy degrees in the J Lounge. The cross-legged burrito guy is reading an article in *Popular Mechanics*. They have a large variety of mags and books. The mags are splayed on top of the shelves containing the books. On top are *Glamour, Good Housekeeping,* the *New Yorker, Referee Magazine.* I think about picking up the *New Yorker*, but I leave it, just like I left the burrito and sit back down to my trusty notebook.

Kick is back. She has moved up a row. I wonder if this was a conscious choice. I have a better angle now on her phone.

She is playing a game where she is offered letters to place in a puzzle that looks like a crossword. It looks like *Words With Friends*, but it's not; it's something different. Her feet are really on the move, at all times. Now it's the left foot, doing a kind of circle dance. Now it's the right foot, tucked behind the left, doing an ants-in-the-shoe up-and-down motion. Now both feet are on the floor, heels bouncing. Back to the left foot tuck. It changes every fifteen seconds or so.

There are not many convos now. The old and young Yukkers are still at it. HLAT and SDak are bantering back and forth about LA Fitness and losing weight. I estimate there are maybe five convos total, all in low voices, creating a low murmur amongst all the coughs and shifting bodies.

I get up to confirm: Yes. There is actually a magazine called *Referee*. In the corner, alongside the bottom shelves, a young woman is sleeping on the floor. She has a laptop plugged in and a purse, so the total surface area she occupies is considerable. I make a joke to myself about waking her up to look on the bottom shelves for a book, but I don't make myself laugh.

10:06. A woman comes to the podium. Everyone sits up or at least looks up. Or most everyone; the girl on the floor is out. At the podium it is announced that we have a fifteen-minute break, which is interesting, because it's not like we're really doing anything. It's a break from waiting, I guess.

I get up during the break for another pee. Everyone is very polite as far as door-holding in the restroom is concerned. The man who arrives at the stall next to me hocks an impressive loogie. It is likely the most interesting sound I will hear all day. He is an older man with glasses and neatly combed, graying hair. When I am back in my seat, I watch him exit the restroom, walk east down the far aisle, and throw something away in the garbage can in the southeast corner, the one under an unwatched TV. Then he walks back up the aisle and, heading north, exits the J lounge. Why did he walk to that particular garbage can?

When he is gone I imagine a writer's convention somewhere. It would be interesting to have that guy come in and reproduce his hocked loogie, then have all the writers describe the sound. Mine would go something like this: It was a growl, wild but loosely constrained, deep, violent, but also efficient. The large wad of phlegm hit the chrome urinal with a loud splat.

HLAT has the *LA Times* open but is still chatting. SDak's daughter is homeschooling her boys. HLAT listens raptly. She is a good listener, nodding along with a frozen smile.

"—that might stimulate your brain," SDak says, and HLAT laughs. HLAT is asking questions, so it's not like she's annoyed and would rather be reading. I think she is enjoying the company. Maybe she's lonely. She keeps the smile on her face. I notice that SDak is providing most of the personal information. I make the judgement that she is one of those people who can talk to anyone, about anything. The muscles on HLAT's face are engaged, holding the smile in place.

Kick is back, now immediately across from me again, making me think her earlier decision to move up a row was unconscious. Nod is a few seats down from her. He is back on his phone and looks a little bored.

There is another young person sleeping on the floor, along the front row, in the third section from my seat, near the unwatched TV.

HLAT has put down the paper and is using her hands to talk. She also plays with a ring on her middle finger.

Kick's right foot is really going, thumping like a rabbit. The chess game is over and the two friends are talking, with bursts of loudness, but they are just far enough away and there is just enough background noise that I can't really make out what they are saying. Their conversation and mannerisms are markedly different than the other interactions due to the fact that they presumably know each other. The Yukkers and HLAT/SDak are having polite conversations with a stranger. These two are friends, goofing around.

Across the J Lounge is a banner, not quite taut on the wall:

JURORS:
SERVING JUSTICE
SERVING THE COMMUNITY
THANK YOU FOR YOUR SERVICE!

There are also large framed black-and-white historical pictures on the walls. I need a stretch, so I go on a little tour of the photos with my trusty notebook.

The first one, above the magazines, is from 1960 in Vista, California. There is a windmill, a small pond, and a farm with several grain storage devices along rows of maybe chicken coops. Some kind of animal, anyway.

The next one, above the chess pieces, is a 1950 Vista avocado grove with large cumulus clouds hovering above the landscape.

I walk south, past the podium with the California state seal behind it and one flag on each side: US and CA, respectively. Then past the guy sleeping and the unwatched TV, to the south wall. The first picture here is of the Vista Inn. It might be from the '30s or the '40s, based on the car that is sitting in front (my ignorance of both cars and farming being revealed here along with the descriptions of the black-and-white photos).

Next to the picture of the inn is a pic of the pier in Oceanside, probably also from the 1930s based on the automobiles. The picture is taken from above, but I don't think from an airplane.

The height is maybe like a ladder on a firetruck. I want to look more closely, but I would have to walk past two people in an aisle. Plus, I'm somewhat conscious of being the weird tall guy looking at photos and writing in a notebook. Next to the pier photo is the banner.

I'm standing behind Blue, along the back, west wall. Sunlight has started to stream through the four evenly spaced windows along the east wall of the J Lounge. Blue is standing, leaning against a very clean granite counter. The J lounge is an immaculately clean place. The whole counter is granite, down to the floor. The blinds on the windows, from north to south, go from 100 percent total sun, to 60 percent sun with some dappled shadows, to 40 percent sun with more dappled shadows, to 15 percent sun with mostly shadow. The shadows are from the trees directly outside the windows. It's pleasing to watch the shadows stirring and shifting in a light breeze.

One reason I knew the directions, before the sun appeared, is because there is a sign outside the court complex that says, "JUROR'S USE SOUTH ENTRANCE." The first time I had to do J duty, I used the north entrance. Sort of like the Civic Center exit this morning, I am learning from my mistakes, slowly accumulating J service knowledge and expertise.

A man walks out of the restroom while I am standing watching the shadows. He is carrying a Heavy Duty Binder. It's a seriously BIG-ASS binder, very full of papers which I assume are related to his profession. It certainly *looks* professional, but what if it's not? What if it's full of maps for *The Legend of Zelda*? Or porn? If you wanted to conceal porn, I think, that binder would certainly do it. That would be not only strange, though, considering the age of computers and smartphones, but also kind of sad if someone was so addicted to porn they needed to carry it around all the time in a big binder. To cheer myself up, I think it would be ironic if Heavy Duty Binder and Double Big Gulp were put on the same jury, right next to one another, and both his binder and her cup/bucket would have to contend for space.

Megan texts me back. She is also incredulous about the diaper station. Dutch texts me too, congratulating me on my 5-0 week in NFL Pick 'ems. He was 4-1 thanks to a 49ers collapse against Arizona. I respond on our conversation, nicknamed Fantasy Quorum, with a joke about betting against Jimmy, a reference to an earlier remark that Dutch made. Jimmy shares the name of the Arizona quarterback and the third party on the Quorum.

· · ·

I am writing near the west wall when the assistant on the cart comes motoring out. She asks me to stay and just hold open the gate to the counter. I realize, moments later, that this door with a little latch lock must be an inconvenience for her every time she comes to the podium or goes to the bathroom. I watch her and listen to her motorized drive to the restroom.

A woman at the counter smiles as I make a joke about being a doorstop and having a purpose.

"I think some of us are about to get called," she says.

"About that time, huh? It takes a while for the dust to settle," I say back.

"Yes. And I've been eavesdropping."

"Oh?"

She doesn't say anything more, so I go to pee again to be on empty in case I'm called. The bathroom is well-stocked: paper towels and bright pink soap. When I exit, on the way back I am in sync with the assistant in the cart. I hold the door and ask if she would like it closed as she drives by me.

"No, it's fine," she says.

10:44. I walk back to my seat. Kick is MIA. SDak and HLAT are still chatting. HLAT's mouth is still in the frozen mask of a little smile. This must be a face/mask she uses to listen to people, encourage them to speak. I watch as the smile breaks into a big grin at something SDak says. The smile is like a little sign: Talk to me, trust me, I am your friend. Nod is reading a book, probably from the shelves. He is reading from the middle.

I set down my trusty notebook and pick up the *Nation*. I note that it has been in print since 1865. The first section is called "Asking for a Friend," by Liza Featherstone. A 32-year-old woman writes a letter seeking advice on how to find a life partner to have kids with who is also looking for an open relationship. She "feels monogamy is antithetical to the type of feminism and anti-capitalism" she subscribes to. All the decent men she's dated are opposed. The letter is signed, "A Marxist Feminist Slut."

Liza replies, "Dear Slut," and says, "Yes! There are better options!" She gives her some practical advice, mostly in regards to her profile on the social media dating front, and closes with, "Hang in there!"

On the page where Liza's advice continues, there is an adver-tisement for a greener funeral. It says, "Preserve the Earth, Not Your Body." There is a pic of the Earth from space and, presumably, a more environmentally friendly casket that appears to be like some kind of wicker basket construction. The wicker coffin with flowers is positioned in a field of tall grass. It seems to be positioned on a tree stump, though the stump is obscured by shadow, giving the appearance that the casket is floating. Next to the casket it says, "Plan Now."

Tomorrow is Halloween. My daughter Mazey, who woke up

at 6:12 this morning, just as one-year-old Delaney was finally about to doze off, is very excited. "Tomorrow is Halloween!" she kept shouting. Then, at 7:15, when I was irritated and unable to find my wallet, she repeatedly shouted in an unrestrained seven-year-old voice:

Trick or treat!
Smell my feet!
Give me something good to eat.
If you don't
I don't care
I'll show you my underwear!

• • •

Almost 11:00. The eavesdropping woman is still at the counter. Her earlier intel regarding some of us being called soon doesn't appear to be accurate.

One seat over is a white-haired, bearded dude with glasses playing baseball on a device. His clothing and shoes suggest comfort. His hair is long and thick and reaches his shoulders. From his appearance, I would say he's a pretty easygoing guy. He has been at baseball the whole time. His device comes in like a little purse of a bag that has a wolf sticker on it.

Kick is nowhere to be seen. HLAT and SDak are still chatting pleasantly, HLAT with her smile. She has a brooch on her jacket.

11:02. An announcement. Fates have been decided. Maybe the eavesdropper's intel wasn't all that bad. It will be a five-day trial. The woman on the cart announces names in alphabetical order. My heart rate increases as she approaches M. I also feel a slight tingle and perspiration in my palms.

Nod reads during the roll call, not looking up from his book.

Everyone else does what I did: They put down what they're
doing and sit up to attention.

My name is called. It is a long list of people.

LEAVING THE J LOUNGE

We walk languidly out of the J Lounge like cattle, making our
way to the north building. I see Heavy Duty Binder, but no
sign of Double Big Gulp. SDak is here, so I wonder, as I take
small steps down in the hall, if HLAT will go back to the *LA
Times* or *Hamlet*. This is a perfect opportunity for a prankster.
Someone could jump in front of this group, say, "Follow me!"
and the whole herd would just follow them to wherever. Maybe
they wouldn't even have to say anything, just go to the front
and walk authoritatively and, sure enough, it would be like
the pied piper. We turn and turn again, zigzagging through
a hall, so that we are still going north. Then we turn west and
sit down in a hallway. I assume we are in the right place.

Double Big Gulp is here! I don't see her beverage, but I see
her scarf. Glancing down the hall, I see Blue and the woman
who was sleeping earlier. We are all quiet in the hall except
for one woman. She is wearing a short pink and black dress
and high black boots. She is probably around sixty-five. The
woman she is talking to is roughly the same age with short
hair, glasses, shorts, and sensible shoes. Pink Dress is doing
most of the talking. Most everyone else sinks back into phones
or devices, though some people are just staring at the floor
or wall, standing around. I sit down on a bench. The guy on
the bench next to me is wearing a Grateful Dead T-shirt and
jeans. He is staring into the tile floor.

I text Megan that I was chosen. Just then Jimmy responds
to my AZ QB joke. "Miller, get a job." I tell him I'm serving

J duty and that it is very fecund writing matter. I think he will maybe laugh or at least roll his eyes at the term "fecund." Two guys in suits walk by. Back here, in the bowels of the court building, clothing is the real divider, appearance-wise. People are in either suits or plain clothes. Most of the suits, I'm assuming, are attorneys. The two guys make their way down the hallway. One of them has very loud shoes. There is a Hispanic guy standing along the wall directly across from me. He has a dark black mustache, dark black hair, crisp dark blue jeans, a tucked-in shirt, and the general appearance of someone that has his shit together. Not really going out on a limb to say he is probably no stranger to hard work. GD T-shirt is leaning forward and lost in the tile.

The woman on the bench next to me, also likely in her sixties, in a short frayed jean skirt, is reading a book called *Life After Darkness*. A woman, likely an attorney, walks by in very high heels. Someone comes out of the door and asks for the envelope she's holding. "Sorry for the delay," she says. Another attorney walks by in a suit. These attorneys are dressed to the nines. His shoes are loud too. Megan texts me back: "Dayum. Act Crazy." I reply: "I ain't got no babies!" This is a reference to a *COPS* episode I watched back in the day with Richard Sniadecki which featured someone whacked out on drugs getting arrested and telling the cop over and over again, in a high-pitched, drugged-out way, that he ain't got no babies!

We are still waiting in the hall. GD T-shirt has his head in his hands, like maybe he is very tired or hungover or just bored. The Hispanic guy, who I decide to call No Stranger—his jeans are in very good condition. No frays or dirt or anything. Maybe they are new.

We are called into the courtroom. The first thing I notice is how bright it is. It has very strong fluorescent lighting and nice framed pictures of nature around the walls: A white seal in snow. A polar bear, turned toward the camera. The Grand Canyon at sunset (or maybe sunrise?). We file in very slowly with a collective small languid shuffle. Someone is holding the door open. The attorneys are standing, facing us. The defendant is a young bearded guy in collared shirt, also standing but not facing us. The prosecutor is a young woman with long dark hair. The defense attorney is a middle-aged guy with glasses.

On the way in, I noticed Double Big Gulp drop her large bucket of a beverage in the garbage by the door of the courtroom, still with some soda remaining—maybe three good sips, warm though. My tired brain tells myself a joke: Wait! Are you going to drink that? I only had a Single Big Gulp this morning!"

I see Heavy Duty Binder carrying his big-ass binder into the Jury Box. We are instructed by a clerk to "sit anywhere" as they will place us in seats momentarily. My brain is on a hot streak, humor-wise, and I imagine myself taking the judge's seat. "You said sit anywhere!"

Besides the clerk, a court reporter, the defendant, and the attorneys, there is also a very serious-looking bailiff in the room. His mustache rivals No Stranger's. Very dark and full and smooth. Maybe they comb them?

Behind the judge's bench there is the California state seal, along with a US flag and a California flag. There are two plants on top of shelves off to the side of the courtroom. This sounds mean, but the clerk looks rather froggish: She is short with thick glasses and very little neck. The judge enters and we all rise.

He goes through his spiel and uses a friendly, professional tone with a few jokes sprinkled in. He gets a laugh only once though, when he kids about Juror #1 being the most qualified. There are fifty-seven Potential Jurors, sixteen of whom will be selected. We look around and realize our odds. Then we are told where to sit. The froggish woman, much like the clerk in the J Lounge, struggles with names. I don't have to move. I am in the back row, just like last year, beyond the Box Next To The J Box. I am potentially a Potential Juror. None of the people I have identified in this here narrative are in the J Box. Some, like No Stranger, are in the rows designated for Potential Jurors, the Box Next To The J Box. The others, like Double Big Gulp and Heavy Duty Binder and GD T-shirt are all like me, Potential Potential Jurors. I look over and see Kick, still working the feet.

The judge continues with his spiel. Writing an "SOS in the J Lounge" essay is all fun and games, watching curious human beings and the rolling slow heavy-wheel process of jury selection, that is—until charges are read. Then it gets serious in a hurry. The judge reads the charges: The defendant is charged with kidnapping an eleven-year-old girl. This news has a sobering effect on all the Potential Jurors, regardless of seating. Suddenly the bailiff's expression makes perfect sense.

During the judge's spiel, the defense attorney asks to approach the bench. Both attorneys rise and the judge gets up and they go off into this little room, like they are stepping backstage for a moment. While they are out it is dead quiet; the bailiff, with his serious expression—a real poker face—is looking at us in a 100 percent neutral way that also says, "Don't even think of screwing around in this room!" The froggy clerk is doing work on her computer and the court reporter closes her eyes.

Suddenly, the defendant turns and breaks the silence. One of his eyes is messed up. "How is everyone doing this morning?" But the froggy clerk shuts this down ASAP. The bailiff doesn't even have time to react. The judge comes back and we are dismissed for lunch. Before letting us go, he reminds us of what he said earlier: We cannot discuss the case with anyone until it reaches its conclusion. This includes the attorneys (which the judge assures us are very nice people), the other Potential Jurors, our families, etc. A good name might be the Hush-Hush Policy.

Oh, one more thing: There is a couple in very nice clothes, dispelling the whole, everyone-dressed-up-is-an-attorney theory, standing in the back of the courtroom, right by me, touching the entire time. Sometimes they hold hands. Sometimes he has his arm around her. They have very serious expressions, and I can only assume they are the parents of the victims.

• • •

Back in the hallway after lunch. Waiting to get back in. Got my badge on, a transparent piece of plastic containing the perforated square of paper that came attached to my summons. It has a number and a bar code. I have a cup of iced coffee and I am looking at the familiar faces, including Blue. I am sitting on a bench across from a man wearing a beanie next to a guy with the bill of his hat turned up. If you could replace the drab wall behind them with a beach, it could pass for a SoCal postcard. The man next to me has nice brown leather dress shoes with blue laces. Even with the coffee, I am feeling the effects of sleep deprivation, so maybe it's time to tuck away my trusty notebook for the day, to power down and let my brain float inside my head until we get back in. I'm where I'm supposed to be. On time. Waiting.

• • •

The afternoon session kicks off and the judge starts in on the questionnaire: twelve questions for the Potential Jurors in the J Box and the Potential Jurors in the three rows directly behind and facing the J Box. The J Box has sixteen seats, and like all the J Boxes on TV, faces the courtroom like stands on a tennis court for a direct view of the action. The Potential Jurors and Potential Potential jurors are seated in rows that face the judge and the backs of the attorneys, with the only difference being the Potential Potential Jurors are sitting in the back row or the rows behind the defense, which, after thinking for a moment and retracing my steps, I believe to be the east side of the courtroom.

Side note: This morning, as I first scribbled down my SOS in the J lounge thoughts and observations, I had mistaken east and west, somehow turned around, until I saw the sunlight and the shadows on the windows. It made me think of how you can live with false beliefs or understandings of The Way Things Are. Like way back in the day people thought the world was flat or the Earth was the center of the universe. Then they were confronted with the fact that there are moons that orbit Jupiter. Or they see something like the mast of a ship slowly sinking beyond the horizon. A pancake-shaped Earth seems ridiculous today, but two thousand years from now, if people haven't destroyed themselves or the planet, I'm sure they will smirk at how naive we are today. But the point is that the way you think or see is inaccurate, somehow. Until you see something that changes what you believe—in my case, literally, the light.

• • •

Back to the courtroom: Before launching into the questions, the judge gives us a strong admonition about social media: Don't post or tweet anything about the case. He gives a couple examples of a juror posting each night on Facebook the details of the case and everyone commenting on it, and how this came to light later and they had to redo the whole trial. Or another one with a juror tweeting the vote count in the juror's room as the jury was deciding. Again, they had to do a whole new trial, at the expense of John Q. Taxpayer.

The questions start off standard: Name. Occupation. Children. Do your children live with you? Have you ever served on a jury? Have you heard about this case in the media? And then it gets personal: Have you ever been convicted of a crime? Know anyone in the criminal justice system? Anyone in your family a victim of a crime? Reasons you can't serve. Can you be fair?

One of the interesting ones is that one about having served on a jury. If you have, the judge wants to know if you were you able to reach a conclusion. He doesn't want to know what that conclusion was; he just wants to know if a verdict was reached. If not, he wants to know why.

My funny bone chimes in with humor in the style of *Airplane!* (or *Hot Shots!* (or another classic, *The Naked Gun*)) and imagines a juror forgetting this and saying that he found someone guilty, with the judge putting his fingers in his ears at the key moment and shouting, "LA-LA-LA-LA-LA-LA" so he doesn't hear.

Out of the fifty-seven people, roughly thirty had the questionnaire waiting for them on their seats when they got back from lunch. The judge goes into his spiel about how to answer the questions. His directions are very specific with two main goals: to move through the questioning period as efficiently as possible, and to do the very real business of providing the defendant with a fair and impartial jury. If you had an axe to grind, this isn't the place.

The judge looks like an actor, Jason Sudeikis, except maybe about ten years older with thinning hair. He maintains his friendly, polite, professional demeanor during the questioning phase. Easygoing, almost like he is meeting a group of people for happy hour. He seems to enjoy this part of the work, the variety and eccentricities of humans. It's sort of a balancing act between his curiosity and the task at hand. Sometimes he makes little jokes or friendly comments. For example, Juror #7 (all the Jurors and Potential Jurors have numbers, while the Potential Potential Jurors like me are numberless) has three children: a doctor and two engineers. The judge says, "Wow, so they are doing very well for themselves!" Juror # 11 discusses a business trip he has next week that will cost his business some cashola if he has to reschedule. The judge asks, "Where are you going?" Juror #11 says China. "Well, have a nice trip," the judge says, after dismissing him.

The judge also shows his human side in another way, going out of his way to tell us that our comfort is important, so if we need a break or if we have to use the bathroom, we can raise our hands and he will call a recess. Juror #14 tells the judge he has recently had knee surgery, saying it was "bone-on-bone" for a while. The judge winces and asks if he is sure that he can serve. "I think so," #14 says. The judge tells him he can stand at any time if it would be more comfortable.

The presumed parents of the victim are back, and he has his arm around her again. They are young and still very serious.

•••

The ceiling has five rows of six square fluorescent lights. It is like a dance floor or a BINGOO (with an extra O row) card on the ceiling. When someone says something vague or evasive or ambiguous, the judge looks up at roughly the G4 square, cocks his head, squints one eye and digs in: "So, when you say [blank] what do you mean by that?" He looks them in the eye, lets them answer, and then, with eyes back at G4— or maybe G6—he repeats it back to them: "So when you say [blank], does that mean that you won't be able to be fair and impartial in this case?" He has like a sort of radar that catches anything suspicious or irregular or just plain vague. Another example: "So does that mean something that happened fifteen years ago in Santa Barbara, might come back and influence you in this case, even though it clearly has no bearing?" Juror #9: "Yes, I think it would." The judge (eyes back at G4): "How exactly does that have a bearing on this case? Can you explain how that incident fifteen years ago in Santa Barbara with your boss might influence you now?"

The other thing is that you have to say "Yes" or "No." There can be no uh-huhs or nods or any other kind of affirmation or negation. This is for the court reporter. Everything has to be on the level, recorded with accuracy.

• • •

The courtroom has a stained glass window from the original courthouse in San Diego hanging high on the west wall. There is a plaque that explains that the window is the state seal of Minnesota and was made by an artist in San Francisco in the 1890s. There is a man in a cowboy hat with a plow, a Native American on a horse, the sun rising, and a river rushing alongside the whole scene. This artist made forty-two windows, one for each state at that time. It is very beautiful and I wish it were on the east wall in the J Lounge, so I could see the sunlight with the shadows of the trees hit it, instead of in this courtroom with no windows.

• • •

Juror #1 does a real botch job with the questionnaire. It is like he did not listen to one word of the judge's directions, which is especially surprising because he is #1 and the judge specifically mentioned that we would go in numerical order. For example, the judge says that if your answer is "No" for anything, you need to say the number, like: "Three—No. Four—No. Five—No." Something like that would be acceptable. However, if any answer is a "Yes," you need to explain. Well #1 does a real botcheroo. He sort of meanders his way through, like the judge is going to be fine proceeding through this all willy-nilly.

"Yeah. No. Yeah. No. No. Yeah."

"Wait wait wait," the judge says. "Was that Yes for number four?"

It goes on like that, with the judge having to repeat his instructions. "And did you reach a verdict?"

"Yep. We found him guilty."

"OK," the judge says. Then he has to say again, "Again, I don't need to know the verdict, like innocent or guilty; I just need to know if you were able to reach one." He shows a lot of patience and not even a hint of exasperation, whereas, little old me, sitting in the back (without my trusty notebook—I don't think the bailiff would let that fly), wants to give a good solid audible smack to my forehead. It gets worse, too, with #1 because there's something about his daughter, who apparently doesn't live with him (though the picture is somewhat murky and the judge, after several glances up to G6, finally decides to move on). Anyway, his daughter apparently had some incident in a restroom at Palomar College. #1 acts like this is the reason we are all gathered and that he is not in the J Box but on the witness stand. The judge has to play attorney and really dig to get at what exactly happened. It's not a good start, but the judge is a pro. It's nothing he hasn't dealt with before, and finally we are on to Juror #2.

• • •

We get moving, and some dirty laundry comes flying out. #2 does cyber security for the Navy. He can't talk about it. The judge jokes about this good-naturedly and moves along. The convicted of a crime question really turns up some doozies. DUIs. Busted for growing pot in the '80s. Pink Dress had fifty charges of felony fraud reduced to a misdemeanor (something about falsifying records for a construction company). Someone else, insurance fraud. Also, the family- and-victim-of-violence question turns up some rather unsavory business. Juror #7 has a brother who has been in and out of jail more times than she can count. She doesn't think she can be impartial. The judge goes to his ceiling light and really sorts through the why and the how. "So if I'm understanding it right, you feel because your brother. . ."

• • •

I am sitting in the back row very much like the plant across from me on the shelf. We are both alive, and our active participation is roughly equivalent. Neither of us has spoken. My mind is a little tired and makes a tired joke about the plant objecting. Everyone in my row is watching the questionnaire exchange between the judge and the Potential Jurors like a tennis match, their heads turning to follow the action.

• • •

The accused sits very still, staring straight ahead. I wonder how he feels about the easy banter and light laughter. Juror #28 is a student and he has an exam on Wednesday. He's young, early 20s.

Judge: Why didn't you postpone your jury service?

#28: I don't know.

Judge: So you just kind of rolled the dice that you wouldn't be selected?

#28: Yeah.

Judge: Well, you lost. Please return to the jury lounge to reschedule your service.

#28 walks out of the courtroom with an "aw shucks" expression, almost like someone had told him, "Just go, you won't get picked." And now he couldn't wait; the first thing he was going to do after rescheduling his service was to call this friend and debunk their shoddy advice.

• • •

Periodically the judge has to remind Potential Jurors to say "Yes" or "No." One guy kind of clucks a couple of times.

• • •

During the process a couple of people are dismissed for emotional reasons. One guy is a superintendent of a school district and his daughter's friend was kidnapped and killed. He says he thinks he could be impartial, he hopes he could be. His voice fills with emotion. The judge lets him go.

• • •

Every time a Potential Juror in the J Box is dismissed, a Potential Juror from the Box Next to the J Box replaces them. The clerk calls a new name, and that person fills the empty seat. The judge moves on to the next Potential Juror, telling the recently added person to review the questionnaire and informing them that they will go next. The superintendent was the last Potential Juror in the Box Next To The J Box, so the judge calls out to the Potential Jurors in the Box Next To The Box Next To The J Box and says, "I have to put you guys on the spot." I keep sitting like a plant in the back row.

After the questionnaire phase, the defense attorney rises and introduces himself. He makes some pleasantries and informal comments, then gets right down to business. He questions the roughly thirty Potential Jurors in the J Box and the Potential Jurors in the Box Next To The J Box, standing near the bench in a very neutral and open way, using a calm voice. He doesn't go in order but rather bounces around. He has a wide sheet of paper with a sticky note for each Potential Juror on which he recorded their answers to the questionnaire.

At one point he questions Juror #11. "The defendant was found to be masturbating in his cell. Would this influence your opinion or in any way cause you to feel a bias against him?"

#11 answers soberly that "No, I don't think so."

The defense attorney hones in on two issues: if it would upset people to hear the testimony of an 11-year-old girl, and whether you can tell intent. Masturbating doesn't come up again. If I was #11, I'd be like, why did I get the masturbating question? The defense attorney asks, "How would you know if someone intended to do something?" There are several scientists in the crowd who discuss evidence. The answers vary widely. He sifts through it all carefully. "How could you be certain?"

• • •

The defense attorney revisits some of the unusual things that came up during the questionnaire, like #1 and his daughter's bathroom incident. It drags on until after 3 p.m. The prosecutor watches it all, making little notes on her own wide page covered with post-its. She keeps glancing at the clock. Around 3:30 the defense rests and the prosecutor stands and does the same formal introduction but also informal asides. She makes a joke about having to speak last, at the end of the day, when everyone is tired. People smile in a mirthless kind of polite way. She doesn't get far, though. Pretty soon it's 4:00 and the judge calls it a day. All the people in the Jury Box, the rows of Potential Jurors, and the rows of Potential Potential Jurors are expected back in the courtroom at 9:00 a.m. tomorrow. We are reminded not to talk about the case or post anything on social media.

• • •

I get in my car and drive home, singing to the radio, feeling good about myself, like I do after a day of teaching, like I've made a small contribution, about eight hours' worth, to the Greater Good.

• • •

Day 2, 8:55. We are back. The same faces and bodies and expressions and mannerisms, just different clothes with the lone possible exception of the judge's robe. The door opens and we file in with the little steps of a bottlenecked group. All the Jurors and the Potential Jurors have assigned seats that correspond to the attorneys' pages with sticky notes. The Potential Potential Jurors all are each allowed to choose a seat amongst the back row or the rows behind the defense. I'm caught in the middle of the flow, so I end up on the right side, squeezed in the middle of a row.

• • •

The prosecutor is joined today at her desk by another attorney. A large young Asian guy. He is a big, not only tall but sizable. It is genetic and not like an overweight thing. He has big bones, wide shoulders, a thick neck, and bulky limbs. His suit jacket bulges. His head is enormous. I can't imagine he could ever rent a helmet. He sits and takes notes and doesn't ever say a word.

I glance over and see that Kick is wearing different shoes. The pink striped canvas shoes with an emphasis on comfort are gone. Today she has gold sparkly flats. Also, she has a foldable fan so that, in addition to the kicking, she fans herself in the same kind of anxiousness nervousnessnessness pattern.

The prosecutor picks up where she left off and gets right back into the whole deal about whether you can tell intent. "How can you tell if someone intends to do something?" Jurors and Potential Jurors are called on like kids in a classroom. She has made some error with her sticky notes and twice uses the wrong name, but she is not in the slightest embarrassed. Rather, it's an opportunity to use some good old self-deprecating humor.

She doesn't spend nearly the same amount of time questioning Potential Jurors as the defense. She wraps up, and we are dismissed for a ten-minute recess. Walking out I see Double Big Gulp has a fresh drink. There is even a ring on the carpet from where her drink has been. Like me, she is a Potential Potential Juror.

The non-juror young couple who appear to be the parents of the victim are back, in different nice clothes and always touching, holding hands, a hand on the back or shoulder, etc.

Out in the hall people chat, read, scroll on their phones, or, like Kick, do the old stand-and-stare.

We file back in. Someone different always holds the door, and there is a standard of politeness and civility as people shuffle to their seats. This time I avoid the middle of the flow and find the back row to get more leg room. The judge does his little spiel explaining the process and reminds everyone that if you are dismissed it's nothing personal yada yada. Then the attorneys start dismissing people inside the J box. It's a game of musical chairs. When someone is dismissed, a Potential Juror is called in to take that spot. I think of Hawk Harrelson, a former White Sox baseball announcer who used the expression, "He Gone!" when an opposing player struck out. #1 He Gone! #3 He Gone! No one dawdles when dismissed.

During this process I watch the court reporter. Her fingers hover and pounce steadily at the keypad, sort of like that blue-elephant looking creature in the band at Jabba's palace in *The Return of the Jedi*. I am curious about the keypad, as it looks like she touches the pad at a rate of one key per word. I have lots of questions: How many keys does it have? How does it work exactly? How does one go about becoming a court reporter? Does she enjoy the job personally? Her feed is streaming live on the judge's computer screen and he watches it like a hawk, showing the significance of the permanent record being created, the official one, as opposed to this here narration (written in low-tech fashion, with a black pen, I might add). The judge informs us of this in his usual lighthearted, friendly manner: "I'm not playing solitaire up here, in case you're wondering why I'm always looking at my computer screen."

The attorneys are really going at it: Jurors are dropping like flies. Being back-row center I have a good view of the faces of recently dismissed Potential Jurors. Their expressions are peaceful, like the face of someone who has played a part on a stage, but the part is over now, they've done what they can do, they are exiting, going back out into the world and their lives, and looking forward to whatever that may be.

The attorneys continue to hack away. The judge is keeping track. I'm not sure how many dismissals they get, maybe fifteen. The defense does away with a bunch, then the prosecutor takes a turn, then the defense wipes out a few of the new faces, and it goes back and forth. The Potential Potential Jurors, we start to sit up a little straighter, pay a little more attention, as the field of Potential Jurors is almost gone.

On the last Potential Juror, both attorneys rest. All the Potential Potential Jurors heave a collective sigh of relief. That was a close one, our expressions say. It's like a smirk immediately wiped away when the judge says, "Everyone in the back, you're not off the hook yet. We still need alternates." Gulp.

Two names are called by the froggish clerk to go sit in the alternate seats in the J Box. I hadn't realized that the last two seats in the box are the alternate seats. Then four more names are called into the Potential Juror row. My name is the fourth and last name called. Everyone around me has the smirk again, doubled this time. That was a close one. Glad I wasn't called at the very end just when I thought I was safe.

We are given the questionnaires and a minute to look them over. The first two Potential Jurors in the J Box go, then it is our turn in the PJ row. I think real hard about question 12: Is there any reason you can't serve on this jury? I think about playing my three-daughter card, that I won't be able to be fair to this guy in the hot seat, that I will lean toward the prosecution because I don't want him on the streets where he could maybe harm my kids. But I don't play it. "No on 12," I say.

"What kind of writing are you doing?" the judge asks me, regarding my answer to question two, my profession. (I answered writer, since this school year I'm on a leave of absence from teaching to be a stay-at-home dad and, in what free time I have, give the old writing dream a kick in the tires.) "Mostly fiction, some nonfiction. Essays." Then I add, for the benefit of the entire courtroom, including the reporter and the clerk and the bailiff, so they don't think I'm just some hack, "I have an article published in a medical magazine." But I know that I say this for myself. "Congratulations," the judge says. "No crime novels?" he says with that little twinkle of humor in his eye. "Not yet. But maybe someday!" I say. I look over at the court reporter's fingers pressing buttons, wondering if she's typing something like: Alternate #6 hasn't ruled out writing a crime novel.

• • •

Alternate #1 seems like an ideal juror. He works as a manager of a shipping department for a large craft brewery company. "All day long I listen to conflict. It's what I do." Alternate #2 on the other hand, is a sure-fire drop. She says yes to #12. She is a grandmother. She talks about her grandchildren. She plays the card and it is genuine, unless she has some extensive background in drama. She starts to cry. The defense attorney thanks her for her honesty.

After the six of us have all answered, the judge calls for a sidebar conversation. All three attorneys and the clerk go out the back door, once again like they are going backstage.

They are gone and there is a silent stillness, the only sound the hum of fluorescent lights, with the bailiff watching everyone.

I figure I'm still in good shape. I'm Alternate #6. So when #2 is bounced (She Gone!), they have #3, #4, and #5 to choose from before they get to me. #3 through #5 all had pretty vanilla answers.

I look at all the nature pictures. I notice that on the back wall is a picture of a salmon jumping midstream directly into the jaws of a waiting bear. It is probably no coincidence that this is on the back wall, not on the side wall next to the defendant.

The judge and attorneys and clerk all come back in. The judge announces that Alternate #1 (seriously?!) and #2 (no surprise) are dismissed. Then he dismisses #3 and #4, putting #5 and Yours Truly in the alternate seats. Just like that, in the wink of an eye, snatched from the jaws of dismissal, I'm an alternate on a jury. Before the judge dismisses the rest of the Potential Potential Jurors (there are about ten left), he tells them that sometimes the process of selecting a fair and impartial jury requires the court to work through the entire field of candidates. He says that sometimes they even have to call more jurors in from the J Lounge. "So your service was not for nothing and even though you didn't play an active role, your service was equally as valid and important."

I am a little shell-shocked to suddenly find myself up in the J Box, the real thing. I watch all the PPJ's slowly file out with the same expressions of looking forward and now-that's-over. I look back at my plant, wondering what the bailiff would do if I called out to it longingly.

I can tell you about the whole thing now, because it's over.

The case lasts the rest of the day: judge's spiel (read from a thick binder that rivaled the now long gone Heavy Duty Binder). Opening statements. Then in the afternoon the prosecutor calls the mother of the girl that the defendant grabbed. (It's not the woman from the couple in the audience. Now I am wondering who the young, sharply dressed couple touching each other with concerned expressions the whole time are? Maybe a relative of the defendant? I can only speculate. Also, there is one other audience member on Day 2, maybe like a law student that has to attend cases and take notes or something as he has a notebook out and is writing.)

Here's what it's about. This eleven-year-old girl and her mother were riding the bus and the defendant stared at and sort of harassed the girl on the bus. Then he got off at the same stop, followed them, and grabbed the girl's butt. The word "butt" comes up a lot and it's kind of funny in an immature way to see all these serious people in serious clothes and in a very serious situation keep saying "butt." The other prosecutor, the guy with the big head, maintains his silence. At one point, late in the afternoon, I think that he is falling asleep. The defense attorney makes a good case: There was no duct tape, no van, no rope. No intent to kidnap. The defendant is facing some serious charges: kidnapping, intent to do harm to a minor, and one other one I forget.

The mother's testimony is a debacle. She doesn't speak English and has to use a translator. This only adds to the confusion. She is convinced that the defendant tried to take her daughter. Yet she doesn't really follow the questions of either attorney. The defense attorney has to object over and over again, with a majority of his objections being sustained. Each time he objects, he cites the Constitution and some legal codes. It's a mess. There's a video from the bus. The mother is kind of stubborn. There is a whole hour of my life I'll never get back where they try to pin down where the butt grab occurred. The mother gave a different testimony in July, after the event. She lives right by the transit station. They have footage from the bus, from the station, from the 7-Eleven that the girl and her mother ran by and as he followed. It's almost like the mother doesn't know her own neighborhood that well. Everything is a big struggle, even basic things like which street they were on, etc. One example that almost causes Yours Truly to give the old forehead a smack is when she is asked to point out the defendant on the 7-Eleven footage. They keep replaying it, the defendant clearly walking by a minute after she and her daughter are shown running, and yet she doesn't point him out with the pointer. It is an exercise in patience for the judge, but still, he is unflappable and familiar with navigating difficulty in the courtroom. The day ends with her still on the stand. It's clear the mother didn't do anything on the bus, sitting there for something like twenty minutes, in the middle of the afternoon on a crowded bus, while this guy stared at her daughter. I could almost hear the other Jurors thinking: Move! Get away! Don't just sit there! Do something!

• • •

The next day, we all file into our seats and prepare for another day of similar testimony, including the daughter taking the stand.

"There's been a development," the judge announces. "The daughter has decided not to testify. Since she is a key witness in this case, the charges are being dropped."

Just like that, it's over. As quickly as it began. The judge thanks us for our service and we do the same dismissal walk:

We played a part on a stage that is now over, and we can simultaneously feel good about what we have done and look forward to our lives ahead. I give one more glance back at the judge and his striking similarity to Jason Sudeikis, the attorneys smiling politely (but not the one with the big head— he just stares straight ahead), the bailiff with his poker face, the froggy clerk, the court reporter, the back of the defendant's head, and finally the salmon jumping into the bear's mouth.

Out in the hallway, we walk along, unclipping our badges. I overhear one juror say to another, "Well, that's that."

LIQUIDS OR ACKNOWLEDGEMENTS IN THE MACHINE.

PLEASE HANDLE.

Day 1, 8:45 a.m.

"Excuse me, sir, you can't put that mug through the machine. You'll have to hold that coffee, along with your gratitude for Nimmy Dumm of Aspen Root Editing, for her **Herculean** effort."

"But the sign says—"

"Thank you, sir. I know what the sign says. Now move along."

"Sure."

"The water bottle, too, along with your acknowledgement of Vanessa Mendozzi for her typesetting and jacket design. Same with the inspiration from David Foster Wallace's *Consider the Lobster*. None of that can go in the machine."

"All right. Whatever you say."

Day 1, 10:28 a.m.

"Sir, you can't put that mango raspberry smoothie in the machine. Same with your appreciation of Wanda McLaughlin, for her time, reading of early J Lounge essays, and encouragement. Outside the machine, please."

"No problem."

Day 1, 12:45 p.m.

"Hold on there, fella. Don't even think about putting that there soda cup in the machine. I see you got the "other" button punched on your lid. What is it? Dr. Pepper? Unless you went root beer. You one of them root beer drinkers? Most places 'round here have Mug, which I believe does not have caffeine. You look tired, though. Tired as shit. I bet you went Dr. Pepper. It's Dr. Pepper isn't it?

"Yes."

"I knew it. That's the fifth Dr. Pepper today. Pay up Stan. Oh, and that immeasurable debt of gratitude to Pearl Jam for all the shows, mood enhancing, inspiration, and, well, not to overstate things, but it's fair to say they opened your ears to the world of rock and roll specifically and music in general. I mean how many years did you play the riff to "Rearviewmirror" without even learning any of the chords? That's not going in the machine. Not today."

"Sure. I got it."

"Here's your buck, Roger, you win again. What is it with these jurors and their soft drinks? I like Mug. It's refreshing. And I *like* that it's not caffeinated. Too much caffeine and I get all jittery. One strong cup of coffee in the morning is my max. Whoa, buddy, where do you think you're going with that water bottle?

"It's empty."

"Not quite. I see at least half a sip there. Do you know what happens to our machine if it gets wet? Handle that bottle, fella, along with your gratitude to Windy Lynn Harris for her reading and feedback of an early version of your James Patterson essay.

"Fine. Whatever."

Day 2, 8:46 a.m.

"Not only was the cup enormous, but it had one of those swirly straws."

"A swirly straw? That's great. Isn't that just the kicker? I can picture it."

"Yeah but Stan, you should've seen the look on this lady's face. Like her cup wasn't good enough for our machine. Like she wouldn't *dream* of putting her cup inside our machine."

"Stop it. You're killing me. With a swirly straw, too. That reminds me of the time that lady with the Double Big Gulp— wait a sec, bub. Where exactly do you think you're going with that iced coffee?"

"Oh, right, sorry."

"And all your other acknowledgements that you might be overlooking—those don't belong in the machine, either. Jimmy. Dutch for being your fantasy league commissioner. The entire Nils Erik Johansson Memorial League, including the soul of Luke Schneider. The rest of your friends. The little people at ESPN to make the fantasy football app function and never get any recognition for their toil. The employees of the San Diego County Superior Court of California. The tour guides of Historic Rugby, Tennessee. *The Writing Disorder* and *Across the Margin* for publishing your work. Your family."

"And the glaringly obvious one. That one too."

"I'm sorry. I don't follow."

"C'mon pal, quit trying to pull one over on us."

"My wife."

"Of course her, but there's something else you'll regret if you put it into this machine."

"Oh, right. I should acknowledge the reader. Thank you for reading my book."

"Reader-schmeder. I'm talking about your water bottle. It's beady as all get-out."